D0108607

Family Ties, Corporate Bonds

PAULA BERNSTEIN

Family Ties, Corporate Bonds

DOUBLEDAY & COMPANY, INC.
GARDEN CITY, NEW YORK
1985

Consultant News

Quotes from the/interview with William J. Morin and from the article by Stephen Cuthrell reprinted with permission from 1984 Directory of Outplacement Firms, Kennedy & Kennedy, Inc., Fitzwilliam, New Hampshire 03447.

ISBN 0-385-19015-8
Library of Congress Catalog Card Number 82–48695
Copyright © 1985 by Paula Bernstein
All Rights Reserved
Printed in the United States of America
First Edition

Library of Congress Cataloging in Publication Data

Bernstein, Paula, 1933–
    Family ties/corporate bonds.

    1. Organizational behavior. 2. Industrial sociology.
3. Social role. I. Title.
HD58.7.B47   1985   302.3'5

For Bess Richardson, Jarmie Richardson, Paul Skipwith Wolf

Acknowledgments

To those who allowed me to look into their lives and to those who shared their professional experience and wisdom for this book, I am deeply grateful. Some permitted me to use their names; others asked that I change their names and identifying details, which I have done. I am inspired by their generous spirit and their courage in revealing intensely personal memories and sometimes painful insights.

For assistance and encouragement over many months, my special thanks to: Gonnie McClung Siegel, Marcia Cohen, Georgia Dullea, Constance Rosenblum, Bette Greene, Joyce Lippmann, Bryna Millman.

I am indebted to my editor at Doubleday, Sally Arteseros, and to my agent, Charlotte Sheedy, for their advice and guidance, as well as their friendship.

Without the love, patience, and faith of my family—Allan, Richard, Aline, and Paul, I could never have begun, or finished, this book.

Nor could I have written it without Carol Mamara and Nina Tocantins of Dance Emotions and David Silva and Barbara Rosenblum of *A*

Course in Miracles. They truly helped me to keep body and soul together. They continue to do so.

For you, the reader, I hope that this book provides a new concept about the world of work and new tools to understand it. But most important, I hope that this book will help you find your special niche in the office family and perhaps, someday, your place at the head of your corporate family.

Contents

Family Ties,
Corporate Bonds

ONE

Belonging: Creating Family

"I can't work where I can't create family."
—JOSEPH GIORDANO, *authority on mental health*

Although I could not have known it back then, nor understood it, the idea for this book was born when I was fifteen and beginning my first job.

At fifteen I knew about loneliness. My parents had divorced when I was a baby; I lived with my mother and grandmother, who both worked downtown and came home late at night. Much of the time, I was alone, and nearly all the time, I felt alone.

I had no father in my life; no brothers, sisters, or cousins. And, I'm afraid, very few friends.

The year I was fourteen I attended a student journalism conference and fell in love with the newspaper business. I spent nearly a year on the high school paper and dreamed of being a real reporter on a real newspaper. At fifteen, finally old enough to get a working permit, I wrote to the editor of the local newspaper offering him features about people my age—people his paper ignored, I pointed out. To my surprise, he agreed, and he hired me.

I had been working only a couple of months when I sensed that this was not just any job and not just a crucial first job, but something magical with enormous meaning in my life, even if I was not quite sure what that meaning might be. At fifteen that sense translated itself into a feeling of uneasy, unsettling joy. Uneasy and unsettling because I had never felt that joy before.

Today, I still remember that feeling. I remember walking up to the red brick building at 495 Union Avenue, Memphis, Tennessee, on a soft and still September afternoon and pulling open the heavy glass door, hearing the whish of the rubber along the bottom, and smelling the musty smell of old newspapers piled high along the windows, a smell mixed in with the sweet, sticky odor of black ink from the presses down the hall. I remember thinking, "This is the place I belong." I was going to be all right.

Every afternoon and into the night, I would sit hunched over the steel desk in the fiercely bright city room where fluorescent lights burned their reflection into a waxed green linoleum floor. Banging away on the old upright Smith-Corona with its wobbly "e" key, I typed out stories about sorority parties and football games that others my age were attending but I was not. More frequently than necessary, I walked up to Tom, the shy, cigar-chewing city editor, and asked him any question I could think of—for example, if he thought that stories should begin with quotes or if a lead paragraph was too long when it ran over twenty words.

Tom never grumbled about being interrupted, and I sensed that he was pleased to be asked for advice. After a month he was taking me across the street to Tony's for lunch. With our hamburgers he would order two bottles of Schlitz for himself and two Cokes for me. Soon we would be talking about Life.

In another month he was giving me advice on getting noticed by a certain reporter he noticed I noticed ("Don't be too easy to reach") and on persuading my mother that fifteen was not too young to stay out until midnight ("Bring it up every once in a while, but try not to bully her about it").

At the desk next to mine sat Pete, the assistant Sunday editor who took it as his personal responsibility to improve my writing and, at the same time, my appearance. He teased me about ending so many sentences with exclamation points and nagged me about wearing tailored, matronly blue and gray suits. "Makes you look old," he would say. I agreed with him, eventually, about the exclamation points, but never about the suits. Looking older was exactly what I had in mind.

Across the room, usually behind a vase of red roses some bride's mother had sent, Louise and Carole typed stories about weddings and debutante luncheons for the Society Department, where I had to sort the photographs every Friday night for the Sunday paper. Louise, a big, blond woman with big appetite for everything, ran Society like a finishing-school hell-raiser, and warned me never to let "the SOBs on the copy desk" give me any trouble about adjectives. (Society used a lot of them.) Carole, much younger, serious, beautiful in a severe, frail way, with her auburn hair in a tight chignon accenting her sharp ballerina-like cheekbones, patiently answered my questions about unions and closed shops, explaining that without The Newspaper Guild we would be working twelve hours a day with no overtime pay.

I listened and learned from them all: Steve, the Sunday editor who walked like a water buffalo and ordered me never to begin a sentence with "there"; Lew, the aristocratic sports editor who tossed out sardonic comments about the horse show and about horsey people; Daniel, the sly assistant city editor who sent me out on a thirty-minute wild-goose chase to teach me a lesson about getting street addresses right, and Eleanor, petulant and brusque, the only woman on the city desk, a prize-winning medical expert who seethed when they forced her to write about hemlines or, God forbid, shoes! (She had to double as fashion editor, too.)

Three photographers, George, Marty, and Joe, enlarged my world as they described in detail the state of their art and the state of their love lives. They showed me how to pose people in a photo to make it seem that they're looking at each other with their eyes wide open. They also showed me how men think about women. And how much.

Very quickly, I became close to all these new people in my life.

I loved them and I depended on them. I hurried home from school every afternoon to shed my sweater, skirt, and socks for stockings, heels, and that severe blue or gray suit. Tom, Steve, Lew, and Daniel were there for me if I wanted to try out new leads or new opinions; Louise, Carole, and Eleanor demonstrated the frustrations, the risks, and the rewards of working women in the newspaper business (and also told me when I wore too much eye makeup); George, Marty, and Joe let me in on some secrets of the male club and the photographers' world.

That first job lasted five years, until I married and moved away. I felt that never again would I find people as special, nor would I care so deeply about the place I worked.

I was wrong. At newspapers in South Carolina, Tokyo, Westchester County, and New York City, whenever I pulled open the front door, that same blessed joy of belonging hit me, and I developed important attachments to new editors and reporters—attachments, not merely friendships—that last to this day.

As years went by, I puzzled over this phenomenon. Eventually, I rationalized that I became close to the people at work because I had been such a lonely child. To compensate for the emptiness of my childhood, I sought out full, intense relationships at work—even after I married and had a family of my own at home.

But was the explanation that simple? What was I to the people around me at work? Did they need me the way I needed them?

I had been so preoccupied with my own yearning, acting out my own eager desire for close relationships, that I had not thought about the needs of people around me. But one day it occurred to me to look at things from their perspective, to observe their reactions to me and to others. Then I asked myself if what I had experienced as uniquely my own could be true for them too, and if, as human beings, it is natural for us to play out family life at work.

Which led me eventually to wonder: If we do indeed become members of an "office family," do these identities as daughters, sons, mothers, or fathers shape the success or failure of a career?

I have become convinced that they do, especially after my experiences on a suburban newspaper, where I witnessed the consequences of transforming colleagues into family.

In June our old editor retired. The publisher decided this was a fine opportunity to change course, so be brought in a young editor whose morning daily had just forced the competing evening paper to shut down. Henry, only thirty-seven but already described by the trade magazines as "the hottest executive in the news biz," was supposed to turn us around—increase circulation with new giveaways, persuade the expensive boutiques to buy full-page ads, and win the paper some major prizes for feature writing.

Henry looked like Danny Thomas, without the grace and without the smile and certainly without the compassion. His body angled out in several directions and even his nose had a mean twist to it. We soon learned that he tolerated no dissent over subjects on which he declared himself the authority: Democrats, nuclear war, handguns, and women.

Oh, yes indeed, women.

That first week on the job, Henry started in at once to clear out the people he didn't like. The features editor, the night copy editor, and the art supervisor were all demoted, their duties merged into other jobs with different titles.

That in itself is not unusual in the newspaper business, where people and their titles are shuffled around every so often just to keep the game interesting and the players awake. Nor is the ruthlessness with which he did it uncommon.

What was unusual was Henry's failure to conceal his attitude toward women—long after the consciousness of most men (and editors) had been raised high enough to make them hold their tongues, even if they would not change their minds. Henry said exactly what he thought of women at the moment he thought it. During a Features Department meeting, when the female writers griped, as all writers will, about the headlines over their stories, he exploded, "Do you think that you have a right to carry on like this because you're women?"

The next week he vetoed the scheduled promotion of Jane to night city editor because Ellen was already assistant night city editor. "Two women can't get along with each other for very long," he announced.

Those editors he had demoted were all women: the features editor, night copy editor, and art supervisor. In their places (with raises) he put John, Merve, and Al. "Men have more authority," he insisted when I expressed surprise at the fast pace of promotions.

What about talent, job aptitude, or the ability to work with writers and their egos? I felt that the men were no improvement over the women they replaced, and one new editor was decidedly mediocre. Two of the three men privately admitted they were uncomfortable about being made editors so soon after being hired as reporters.

A young copyreader said something that made sense to me, as we all sat around the Dew Drop Inn bar one November night. "You know," Bill reflected, pouring his beer out slowly, "Henry likes women personally, but not around him at work. He worries that they will start crying or fighting with each other, or do something stupid to embarrass him. After all, he's got a couple of daughters and a wife at home and that's enough women in his life. He trusts the men, I think, because they're his kind of people. And heck, maybe he wants somebody to be like a son to him at work if he can't have one at home."

"You may be right," replied Barry, the night editor on the copy desk. "That could explain some things." He had a deliberate way of talking, making his statements sound like 54-point Bodoni Bold headlines.

Yes, I thought, in the flash of sudden recognition. Henry's attitudes toward women had less to do with us and more to do with his present family life, perhaps even his childhood. (He often reminisced about his early life on a farm, and the two older sisters who bossed him around.) If women made him feel weak and inadequate, did any woman stand much of a chance for a promotion or a raise on this newspaper?

Once again, I remembered the roles those editors and reporters had played in my life during my teenage years on the Memphis newspaper and—of course!—the roles I played in their lives as well.

If I had fathers (Tom and Steve), they had a daughter; if I had uncles (Pete, Lew, and Daniel) and an aunt (Louise), they had a niece. My brothers (George, Marty, Joe) had a sister; my big sisters (Carole and Eleanor), a little sister. Did they need me and were they acting out their needs just as I was acting out mine? Why did I form relationships with them and not with some of the others I worked with? Did my need for them fit their needs for me?

Perhaps I had stumbled onto a concept about careers that might explain why personality, style, and rapport so often triumph over talent, hard work, or even having the right connections. If it was true for me and true for them, could it be true for others?

I had to know if anyone else shared these perceptions about working relationships. I began to discuss my theories with friends, asking for specifics: What are things like in your office? How do you see your bosses and your colleagues? How do they react to each other?

My friends responded with startling insights. They recognized the most important figure at work—the man who was the office father. They identified the man who was a son—sometimes the two or three who were sons. Many of the women thought of themselves as daughters—often, as reluctant daughters. Frequently they could name a mother, a wife, a mommy's boy, favorite child, a brat. Most amazing to me, each person knew where she or he fit into this family constellation. Looking back, they also saw the roles they had played at younger ages in earlier stages of their careers.

Yes, they said, now that you mentioned it, a corporation does seem like a family. Not necessarily that one big happy family they like to boast about when they're hiring you, but, just like every family, a hotbed of passion, rivalry, and dreams that build or destroy careers. (Especially in the *home* office.)

I was obsessed with this idea, and began to pursue it further.

The office father fascinated me most as first, and I talked with executives of several corporations, finding that they identified themselves and several men around them in this role. "A corporation will have several types," the president of an advertising and marketing firm said. "You've got your shark, your snake—the poisonous spy, the slitherer —and you've got your tough, but oh-so-gentle type, just as mean and nasty as the next guy, except that he doesn't kick kids or shoot the neighbors. The shark and the snake will want sharks and snakes as children. They will use anyone, including their young, for their own purpose, and they will eat their young if they need to survive."

He described two more types from recent experience. "As I've found out, you've got your nurturing father who selects his children and keeps an eye on them, correcting them when they go wrong and looking out for them all the time. And as I've also found out, you've got your father who uses his power to position his children and then walks away from them, leaving them to sink or swim."

Next, I explored the subject with psychiatrists, psychologists, professors, and management consultants who specialize in corporate behavior.

They saw faces of the family in the workplace, too. In fact, the concept was familiar to most of them from scholarly research journals. How much of the family some of them saw and how they interpreted what they saw seemed to depend as much on their childhood memories as it did on their professional insights. In typical examples, I heard stories about a man who preferred his office son to his natural son, about an executive who left a new employee alone and defenseless with no place to go in the organization, and—in stunning contrast—about a warmhearted patriarch who inspired an entire university department.

One psychologist winced at a still-painful recollection. His father had lost interest in him, he said, "when Dad knew I was not going to follow him and manufacture ladies' shoes for the rest of my life." The father began devoting all his time to the business, staying at work until midnight most nights.

At Christmas he always asked his son to drop by the office party and shake hands with the staff. "I went there one day when I was seventeen and getting ready to enter college," recalled the psychologist. "I stood around for a long time. He ignored me, and gave all his attention to this twenty-five-year-old assistant whom he was grooming to take over the place, and he was so kind, so much the father, to him." To this day, fifteen years later, the psychologist still feels the humiliation.

A management consultant who was seven when his father died could not forget his first job out of graduate school—and the way he automatically gravitated to one tough, older department manager. Six months later, that manager was lured to a larger firm. "I found a replacement father who taught me the ropes, who protected me," the consultant said. "But then, he, too, got a better offer, with more money and more prestige, and left. I was orphaned, abandoned, drifting again, for the second time. Without them, I had nothing; I was nothing. I left as soon as I could find another job."

With another authoritative older man. This time, it happened to be the one who owned the company and was sure to stay. The consultant is still working there.

Some of us may spend years searching for that special relationship at work. Others find it right from the start—as did a university professor who spoke wistfully of his first boss, now retired.

"For over twenty years," the professor recalled, "our department chairman was referred to as everybody's father, simply in terms of the general umbrella of security and quiet that he spread around the entire department. He could dampen any family squabbles, and there were very few of them while he was here.

"Maybe he had a few favorite sons, but one of his great abilities was to convey the impression that almost everybody was a favorite. He tended to develop that attitude toward any new person coming into the department. He was not a very authoritative person, but he was like my own dad, who was much more the benevolent New Testament father, instead of the retributive Old Testament father."

These conversations led me to believe that the child within us lives. Although we may not realize it, or want to admit it, many of us bring our personal lives, with childhood's emotional baggage, to work every day with us, with far greater intensity than we bring work home at night. I believe that the psychiatrist Dr. Karl Menninger was right when he said, "Many people go through life trying to take out on someone feelings that were generated within them as children."

We are all products of a family, of whatever kind, and we are imprinted by those early years when we learned how it felt to have, or not to have, a father, mother, sister, brother, grandparents, aunts, uncles, and cousins. We are forever influenced by the ways we learned to love them, long for them, cope with them, or fight with them. We might have been any one of several types of children—the Good Child (who obeyed parents and teachers); the Bad Child (who resisted authority); the Responsible Child (who took care of others); the Chameleon (who feared rocking the boat and did whatever necessary to maintain order), or the Mediator (who smoothed out the family quarrels).

Whatever child we were, that child lives on within us—but need not hold us hostage. As adults, we do not necessarily remain in these childhood roles. But the memory of them is always inside us, in our guts as well as in our heads. So is our memory of all the adults around us when we were children. When we go to work, we can duplicate these childhood relationships; we can change them to serve us better, or we can create entirely different patterns of behavior based somewhat on our childhood experiences. We do not have to remain what we were in childhood, and we do not have to recreate the adults of our childhood. We can become what we need to become, drawing on our memory banks and improvising at will.

Sometimes we are desperate to recreate a family role we feel comfortable with. Sometimes we play out our old family dramas, seeking to reconstruct what we remember from childhood, and to resolve it. Sometimes we search for a person we need here and now, someone we never had and always wanted—a parent who will be wise and good, or a child who will be smart and grateful.

Those who study family life and those who study corporate life have several theories about all this, none incompatible with the other.

"The family we grew up in, the family that teaches us more than we'll ever know, is our family of origin. And when we leave to make our own way in the world . . . we attempt to recreate that family in the same way," says Mel Roman, Ph.D., and professor of psychiatry at the Albert Einstein College of Medicine in New York City, co-author of *The Indelible Family* with Patricia E. Raley.

But in attempting to recreate our original family when we go to work, some of us try to improve on it by constructing an entirely new situation. Unlike the families we are born into, our new office family gives us a chance to start afresh, to invent a new identity, to give ourselves what we missed out on the first time around—a deep emotional bond; a loving, nurturing relationship, or, in some cases, a domineering, quarrelsome relationship, if we remember the earlier years as too placid.

"To a large extent, there is a tendency to look to the corporation to make up what was absent in the family," Dr. Harvey Barocas, a clinical psychologist and professor at Baruch College in New York City, told me in an interview.

As we discussed this idea, Dr. Barocas explained that the people most likely to make the corporation their family are those who are searching for some kind of validation for their self-esteem, especially if they had an absent parent—absent physically or emotionally. People like me.

"It is a second opportunity to work through some conflicts," pointed out Dr. Barocas, who sees many corporate executives in his private practice. And it is the real family that is reconstituted in the office—even down to the family scapegoat.

Another expert on the emotional health of executives carried the analogy of the family even further when I spoke with him. Dr. Stanley Lesse, psychiatrist and editor of the *American Journal of Psychotherapy,* told me that a large organization is the symbolic "good father" to its employees, who expect it to protect them when they have problems in their work or mental or physical health.

That symbolic father figure, the organization, is then personified by a real flesh-and-blood chief executive—who becomes the idealized father to his employees.

In their unconscious minds, employees see in him "the image of the strong but good and just father who will give love and protection and understanding in return for devotion and service," Dr. Lesse commented. He explained that frequently these employees carry over a childhood expectation that even if they make a mistake or fail to work as hard as they should, the understanding father will forgive them. And among employees at lower levels, the office may represent the original family, "always with the expectations of a higher level of understanding and kindness," Dr. Lesse added. "In some instances, the work family becomes the first real family relationship that some people experience."

Such relationships may be especially treasured now. With divorce rates so high, the corporation may be a more stable institution than marriage and can become one's family, says Dr. Mortimer Feinberg, chairman of BFS Psychological Associates, a management consulting firm, who writes for *The Wall Street Journal* and is the co-author of *Corporate Bigamy,* a book about the dangers of loving your work too much.

In our conversation he pointed out that not too long ago most adults were surrounded by a traditional extended family of parents, grandparents, uncles, aunts, and cousins. Today, most of us live in a small nuclear family, a single-parent family, or as single individuals. The corporation can give us the emotional stimuli provided in earlier times by that extended family.

Although it can serve our emotional needs by serving *in locus parenti,* we need to distance ourselves from it, believes Dr. Feinberg. For the corporation cannot love us back. It makes no lifetime commitment to us, the way a family does—or should.

Yet we expect it to.

When I asked Dr. Lesse about these issues, he also warned about the danger in projecting our family fantasies onto our bosses. "Unfortunately," he said, "children in public schools, adolescents in colleges, and adults in graduate schools are not taught that no corporation or corporate executive loves you, with the you being 'the universal you.' When middle-range executives are passed by, when middle-range or high executives are reprimanded for failures, particularly if the failures attract public attention, most are taken aback and the criticism has superimposed upon it the marked feeling of rejection, a feeling of unfairness, a feeling of abandonment."

True enough. The corporation, whether we look on it as father or lover, cannot love us back like the real thing. Not only that, it always retains its option to kick us out, to refuse to let us go home again. But, on the other hand, the corporation can protect us, challenge us, and nurture us. And the people within the corporation can and do love us, hate us, fight and make up with us, and provide us with the emotional stimuli and sustenance that we require. For those from broken homes and breaking-up families, the symbolic relationships we form with the corporation itself and the living, breathing relationships with people in the office are likely to become as close to family as we can get. Or as close as we want to get.

Jean, a vice-president of a major New York City bank, is one of the "new woman" dynamos created in the wake of the women's movement. Convinced that the financial world offered women more money and better opportunities than elementary education, she resigned her job teaching third grade and took a salary cut to begin anew as a billing clerk. Soon she realized that she needed an MBA to get on the fast promotion track to the division level, and after three years of night school, she got her degree.

Now thirty-eight, and planning to remain childless, she has become increasingly aware that she spends more time with the people in her office than she does with her husband or any of her friends. Because work absorbs her time and energy almost exclusively, she has developed involved, intimate ties to her colleagues in the office, as well as a style of coping that is comfortably familiar to her. When I asked if she had a "family" at work, she knew exactly what I meant.

"My father was a very dominating man, very excitable, and he was always upset," she said. "My mother let him have his way, and did pretty much what he wanted her to do. I guess I learned that in order to have peace, that's what you do. I found that bosses talk a good line about not liking yes-men or yes-women. I found that in reality, though, they absolutely do hate to be argued with. So after my boss has rejected my idea, I say to him, 'Okay, we'll do it your way. Come to think of it, that is a good way of going.' And that is why I have gotten so far so fast.

"What I soon found out was that whether we argued for two hours or whether I capitulated immediately, the result would always be the same. And that was that he was the boss, and we would do it his way. So I figured, why not just let him be right immediately, and save myself two hours of aggravation? Which I found out that most of the other managers had not learned. They would come out of those sessions destroyed, upset, developing ulcers or a drinking problem. But after the first month, I realized that my boss needed to be right and that was my job, to let him be right. As I did that, I kept getting more promotions and raises."

Jean says she feels like "the mommy" with the employees who report to her and this awakens in her a sensation of being very much like her own mother. "I think that part of my job is being the buffer between my people and my boss, like my mother, who buffered the children from my father. I was called on the carpet for that once. I had given raises and excellent ratings to all my staff people. My boss asked, 'Are you a manager or a mother?' I told him, 'These people are outstanding. I hired most of them. They have done a terrific job and saved the bank more money than ever before.' So he let their raises and their ratings stay.

"I really do feel that they are my chosen people. The children I never had. They ask me for advice, just as if I am their mother. And they are fun to be with, intelligent and attractive."

In her professional life on Wall Street, Jean has created herself as she remembers her mother—in a wife relationship to her boss and in a mother relationship to her subordinates, who are the children she does not have and does not want. Her attitudes about pleasing those above her and below her seem to have worked spectacularly well for her, propelling her from clerk to vice-president in six years. However, she also has intelligence, confidence, ambition, spirit, a sense of humor, skills in solving problems with people, and the ability to learn the demands of a new job almost immediately. How could she remain a clerk with all those qualities?

I have known her for ten years now, and I'm not convinced that adopting her mother's "yes-woman" attitude is the main reason she has gotten so far so fast, as she claims. Yet the reliving of family relationships is for her, as it is for many others, a profound need.

Why has Jean become a wife and mother in the office but not a daughter? How do the players find their roles in the corporate drama? Who is likely to become the father and not the son—or the favorite child and not the scapegoat?

Psychologist Roman and others say that families cast their members in roles they never forget, and these roles are "indelibly engraved" in our memories. We replay the parts again and again throughout life whenever we find ourselves in a group. We are drawn to people who play the roles we know best and who let us play our familiar parts.

In their book *The Indelible Family,* Dr. Roman and Ms. Raley claim that sometimes we reject the role we once played as children and choose another role for ourselves. But that role will also be familiar to us because it is one that someone else played in our original family.

"The roles that we and others played in our families of origin follow us for the rest of our lives," they emphasize. "We don't remember just the roles we played or those that our parents played, but those that grandparents, crazy cousins, and others played. And we can often play any of them ourselves."

I believe that it is also possible to invent fantasy roles for ourselves and for others, too—roles that we never acted out as children and roles that we never knew other family members to play. The human imagination has a limitless capacity to create what it needs at the time it needs it.

When I made a family for myself at that first newspaper in Memphis, I invented roles that I had not known firsthand because I knew nothing about family except mother and grandmother. I acquired some of my ideas of father, sister, brother, aunt, and uncle from the movies or radio or from watching the family next door. I invented an idealized family at a time in my life—adolescence—when I needed it most. In much the same way, perhaps, Henry, that suburban editor with daughters at home, created a family of sons at our suburban paper because he needed them at a particularly critical time in his career. Both of us were drawn closest to the people who played the fantasy roles we knew best because we had fantasized them for so long.

When Jean recreates her family, she is repeating her family relationships in the pattern that worked for her mother. She needs to be wife and mother to the family she remembers as much as I needed to be daughter, sister, and niece to the family I imagined.

For people with happier family memories, it is not a particular person but the entire family atmosphere that must be reconstituted in the office, a family atmosphere often treasured for its distinctive cultural values—macho Hispanic, reserved WASP, witty Irish, or, in the case of Joseph Giordano, loyal Italian.

"I can't work where I can't create family," Mr. Giordano observed as we talked in his narrow office with books and papers spilling out from the shelves that covered every inch of wall space. "I've only been conscious of that as I've begun to explore my own ethnic background, and how my growing up an Italian-American continues to influence my life."

Mr. Giordano is director of the American Jewish Committee's Center on Ethnicity, Human Behavior and Communication. Today he feels like "one of the family" working with the expansive and lively personalities around him—but he recalls earlier years in other jobs where he felt isolated around more rigid, repressed people.

An authority on family life and ethnic and immigrant problems in the United States, he was appointed to President Carter's Commission on Mental Health in 1977, serving on the Task Force on Special Populations. In 1979 he was elected chairman of the Coalition for the White House Conference on Families. He is also one of the editors and contributing authors of *Ethnicity and Family Therapy* (The Guilford Press, 1982).

Joe Giordano was the youngest of four children in a tightly knit, third-generation, working-class Italian-American Catholic family in Brooklyn. "I know there is a real sense of family being all-important, that my own individuality was defined more in the context of what I contributed to the family than what I did on my own," he began.

"I still need to recreate that because I think my sense of myself is in relationships and not in isolation. I think that comes out of the family, and my own experience in growing up."

Mr. Giordano acknowledged a need for steady, loving work relationships and a dependence on them once he has created them. "At work, there is a sense of nurturing, of needing. The feeling of group is the feeling of safety, the feeling reflecting back to me cues that 'You're okay, you're all right, Joe.' I need that constant feedback in an environment. Without it, I feel lonely, isolated, alienated, and unstimulated.

"As in my real family, in my work family I get positive feedback. I think I am recreating my family because I will take steps at work to create a group around me. I think I seek out the people who *feel* like family, rather than people who play the characters of mother, father, sister, brother.

"The situation at work allows you, rather than one straight-line relationship—'He is my father'—to see that people have many roles, and that you also play them. So I can think of situations where I have played, or have related to, a father, son, daughter."

Mr. Giordano connects his sense of family identity at work to his Italian heritage pitting insiders against outsiders—or family versus enemy.

"It's interesting. A lot of the idea of family at work is defined by people whom you trust and whom you don't trust. I think this is an especially Italian concept of family. For example, the sense of loyalty—you never, never put down a family person. Particularly in public.

"I would also never do that in my work role. I would not shame, I would not put on the spot, anyone that I felt very close to in work because that would then translate into family. I think a sense of loyalty, of obligation, of putting yourself out for a family member, and a sense of enemies, is very clear in an Italian family. An enemy is someone who wants to bring harm on the family, who is antagonistic."

At times that Italian upbringing leads him to misinterpret a political move as a personal offense in an office situation or on a committee.

"Now I know, and I catch myself doing it, that it comes out of an ethnic thing, where a personal affront is seen as a greater violation than an attack against my role. I take it personally.

"I've never recovered from being attacked in a couple of things I was involved in nationally. At the White House Conference on Families, they were attacking what they thought I represented and I got very upset, even though I knew they were not attacking me personally. In the President's Commission on Mental Health, they were also reacting to my role as a representative of a Jewish organization, and I also took it personally. I felt stabbed. The little voice inside me said to the world, 'We are all in this as a family against the others, and you don't do that. Don't you understand?' "

Mr. Giordano thinks that people play out their childhood family relationships in many ways at work, depending on the situation and on the other people.

"Any situation is a combination of factors. If you have a good relationship with your own father, and your boss is a son of a bitch, you may find it unpleasant, but you won't get hooked into repeating an old pattern. If you had a father who was a son of a bitch, and you meet a good guy as a boss, you may not even recognize him as good, but you'll play out the same old pattern to test it.

"I think it's a reactive kind of thing. If you had good family relationships as a child, you'll probably have good work relationships. If not, well, you may, in emotional maturity, recognize problems you had with your parents or significant others, and then try to recreate more positive relationships. For instance, if you had a lousy relationship with your father, and you get a terrific boss, it almost becomes a wonderful learning experience. But I think that other people will just run over the same pattern and never quite understand why they have problems at work."

We can solve many of those problems by recognizing individual family behavior patterns all around us, changing them when we can, coping with them when we cannot.

Depending on how it is done, the acting out of family roles in the office has the potential to benefit us personally and professionally. We can create relationships that give us what we never got in childhood, what we remember from childhood, or what we want at this special moment. Sometimes we gain a tremendous advantage by encouraging our bosses, colleagues, and employees to do the same with us. At the very least, just distinguishing the patterns and understanding the way people around us play out their roles can make a difference in the way we view them and in the way we view ourselves. It can also change the course of our careers.

On the other hand, the acting out of family roles has the potential to destroy us personally and professionally. That is why we must identify the roles being played by ourselves and others around us.

It is valuable to know, from the testimony of Joe Giordano and others, that you are not the same person all the time, nor should you be; that you can play different roles with different people; that you can grow, change, and rearrange childhood patterns for today's needs, that you are not doomed to relive all of the early misery, nor repeat all of childhood's mistakes.

It is valuable, also, to anticipate future issues that may one day arise in your office.

Suppose your "son" or "daughter" becomes your boss. Or you and your boss want to play the same role with another person. Or you refuse the role that others assign you on the basis of your age, sex, or job status.

How do we get into these roles in the first place? Do we put ourselves into them or do others assign them to us? How long do we remain in the roles and how do we change?

Suppose your "father" locks you into sibling rivalry with a colleague. Or you want to change roles, becoming the Favorite Child instead of the Scapegoat.

These issues lead to others that change the nature of our working lives.

Do some men need to be "fathers" in different ways to different people in the corporation? What effect does this have on the company, its product, and its people?

Why must some people play one role over and over while others maintain a repertoire of roles?

How long can a "son" or a "daughter" remain in that role? Must he or she eventually be replaced by the younger and the brighter? Must the "daughter" always be girlish to her bosses, "forever in pink ribbons and lace," as one still-glamorous, fifty-year-old advertising executive maintains?

Is it dangerous and destructive for a woman to assume the mother role? What, ultimately, is the safest role for a woman in business?

How can we best cope with these role reversals between female bosses and male subordinates: the daughter over the father, the mother over the son, the sister over the brother?

Hardest of all, how do you let go and begin again? How do you divorce your old company and marry a new one?

Finally, what will become of the corporate family tomorrow? In the electronic cottage at home or in a skyscraper on Main Street, we must combine the new technology with changing family roles while we confront the old child still inside us. How will that work? How will we work?

I set out to find the answers in the lives and in the words of the men and women playing starring roles on the corporate stage today.

TWO

The Father:
Leaving His Legacy

"I'm like a father with a child, and I want it to succeed when I'm gone."
—WILLIAM PALEY, *in 1982, announcing his planned resignation in 1983, after thirty-seven years as chairman of CBS Inc.*

Not having a father at home was the key difference in my growing up, setting me apart from my classmates at Miss Hutchison's School for Girls. More than being an only child, more than living in an apartment, more than having a mother who worked.

Even when I was older, so deep was my longing for a father that I invested male editors with far more wisdom and authority than they actually possessed. Eager to please them, I desperately hoped that they would love me for being the "good child" and following their instructions to the letter. Then, of course, I expected them to show their pride in me by praising my writing and giving me better assignments. I was frequently disappointed. Meantime (as I watched disdainfully then but not now) male reporters my age were replaying last night's game with the editors, inviting them out for a beer, and arguing over page-one layouts as equals although they were not.

Do young men understand in some intuitive way that they must compete for the attention of older men? And do older men, having themselves scaled the heights with the same kind of help, feel obligated to pull up a few ambitious, talented, personable young men? Once on top, looking down from above, when do presidents and board chairmen begin to feel that they and their company are one, that they personify the organization that they helped define or create?

These questions rang in my head when I read William Paley's comment in *Time* magazine: "I'm like a father with a child, and I want it to succeed when I'm gone."

But Mr. Paley was not just voicing the hopes and dreams of a father for a vast empire he had built. Whether he realized it or not, he was also voicing a father's hopes and dreams for his corporate son, Thomas Wyman, who succeeded him as CBS chairman.

Mr. Wyman was the fifth of five handpicked heirs Mr. Paley had brought close to the throne, and the only one who finally made it to the top. The four who did not were Dr. Frank Stanton, who retired when he realized that he was not going to succeed Mr. Paley; Charles Ireland, who died in 1972, and Arthur Taylor and John Backe, who (according to industry observers) were both fired by Mr. Paley after he decided that they were too eager to succeed him.

Like every founder of an empire, Mr. Paley also created sons in his own image. The corporate father can choose his sons, discard them if they fail him, and then choose others closer to his own mold. That is the ultimate power, leaving behind one's best and most glorious self to carry on the legacy.

Every corporation has a symbolic parent, usually the father—often so closely identified with it that he *is* the company, as Mr. Paley was CBS. This corporate, symbolic father, usually the chairman or president, is the one person all employees look to for leadership. He sets the tone of the organization, its style, character, behavior patterns.

Individual departments or divisions, and even some offices, may also have symbolic fathers (managers or supervisors) of much less importance.

For most people the corporate symbolic father is the towering presence. He is the authority figure, naturally, but more than that, he is the giver of life in the corporation—practically as well as metaphorically. He defines the corporation by who he is and by what he does—as he defines his employees by the jobs he assigns, the pay he gives, the promotions he awards.

To try to understand the family structure in the organization, I read many books—among them, *The Psychoanalytic Study of the Family,* published in 1921 by the Institute of Psychoanalysis in London and used as a psychology textbook today. In it, psychologist J. C. Flügel draws on the research of Freud and Jung to explain the influences of our early feelings about our parents throughout life:

"The relations of child to parent and of parent to child are so fundamental to all of human existence and human intercourse, that most, if not all, of our mental life, in so far as it has reference to our fellow creatures, is to some extent reminiscent of them, or affected by them. We can never root out from our mind the tendencies connected with this most intimate and essential of human connections . . ."

Dr. Flügel also points out our tendency to transfer obedience from parents to new authority figures: "In the course of an individual's life, the authority over his expressions, activities and general mode of living originally exercised by the parents, passes in succession, wholly or partly, to a number of other persons . . ."

This means that as we grow out of infancy into childhood, we transfer our feelings about our parents to other authority figures: nurses, teachers, principals. Then as adults, we transfer these feelings to police, employers, professional superiors, doctors, religious leaders, and government officials. They may become objects of our childhood rebellion because we see them as stand-ins for our parents; later on in life, says Dr. Flügel, we may invest these same people with the qualities of perfection we earlier attributed to our parents: unlimited power, wisdom, virtue, or knowledge.

Our feelings about fathers, Dr. Flügel adds, center around respect, obedience, and loyalty to authority while our feelings about mothers are connected to the ideas of being nourished, trained, and protected. We often forget this fundamental (but learned) difference in attitude that makes a "command" or "take charge" presence so attractive in a man but often so disturbing in a woman. When most employees think of the word "manager," they still think of a man, discovered Dr. Virginia Schein, former associate professor of organizational behavior, School of Management, Case Western Reserve University, Cleveland, in a recent research study of attitudes toward men and women in high managerial positions.

This one-dimensional thinking about men and women is changing, of course, as the number of women in corporations increases, as the number of children with working mothers increases, and, as a logical result, more flexible attitudes about women and men develop. But for the next few years at least, the men—and especially the fathers—will continue to be the most powerful figures in nearly every organization.

Symbolic corporate fathers like William Paley have also been what I call "working fathers" to "sons" they groomed for succession, or "sons" whose careers they guided. Without these fathers, the corporation could not exist. It is they who light the path to the top for their protégés, point out the obstacles, teach the short cuts to the top, then either stay with the young men on the way up or cut them loose.

In addition to the top symbolic father, each corporation has several of these working fathers. Sometimes, many of them. The working father may be the boss in the office, but not every boss is a father. A father will be a man whose authority and status are recognized by all those around him, a man whose professional superiority is instantly apparent, a man who has special, close relationships with one or several people under him. He is their father by the force he exerts over them, the force of personality and drive and authority. He is a father by the power he holds over them, the power to change lives, the power to reward or reject.

He is also a father because he is acknowledged as a superior being, a leader. His qualities set him apart from all the other men in the office. He commands loyalty and respect. Usually, everybody in the office knows who he is.

These working fathers are more than mentors, although they can certainly be the world's best mentors, in the classic definition of "experienced and trusted adviser." I think that generally, though, wide gulfs of feelings separate fathers and mentors. A father takes a special, paternal, and exclusive delight in a young man or woman. On the other hand, a mentor takes a more detached, more businesslike and less personal interest in a colleague. The difference is in the emotional quality of the relationship.

One morning on the commuter train, I got into a discussion about this with a corporate lawyer. He considered the possibilities and finally decided that although fathering and mentoring were to some extent the same, they branched off at the crossroads of selfishness and generosity.

"In mentoring, you may be looking to feather your own nest for your declining corporate years, so there should be someone there to help you, to look out for you later," Jim, the corporate lawyer, explained as if he were in a courtroom.

"Fathering, I think, would just be a parental impulse, offered without hope of reward. Possibly, because you were not successful with your own children, then other young people came along, and you had things to give that were helpful to them that were not helpful to your own children."

Fathers in corporations usually have one or two sons they take great interest in promoting to the top, but they treat virtually all women as "daughters," rarely singling out one for special treatment. Through history in nearly all societies, sons have been valued more highly than daughters. Certainly at the higher levels of the American corporation, men have been more welcome than women.

Although much is changing for younger corporate executives, the men now in their fifties and sixties have rarely had the chance to be a father to women in the same ways that they have been a father to men. They have not been around many women on that level at work. They have had little opportunity to see women as daughters taking over the reins someday the way they saw men as sons to be groomed for top management—or saw themselves as sons, when they entered the corporation.

Most of them see women as dependent creatures, in the same way that their daughters at home, but not their sons, are dependent on them.

This theory was validated again and again by professionals who shared their knowledge and their personal experiences with me.

Most male managers are still handicapped by their conventional attitudes toward sons and daughters, Dr. Joel Lefkowitz, professor of industrial psychology at Baruch College in New York City, told me. "Whereas a man might not object and, in fact, it might not at all be detrimental to his career to be viewed as a son by an older executive, for a woman to be perceived as a daughter has a pejorative aspect. It conjures up visions of little girl, sweetness, helplessness, and just the kind of stereotypes that work to the disadvantage of an assertive woman who wants to develop a good career in a business organization. But the real issue is that playing the role of daughter is limiting and self-destructive, whereas playing the role of son is not."

As more women enter the corporation and reach higher levels, more men will have daughters as well as sons. Women at the top will have sons and daughters, too—a new issue that will involve considerable shifting of emotional and professional gears.

At this moment, though, the typical response of a working office father to women is the one that I heard from Gene, an advertising sales director for a cable TV network: "I have two women I father, sort of," he said. "I am most involved with their social and personal lives, not their business careers. I think women have a hell of a lot more problems. They are not oddities in the office anymore, but they are still violating a whole lot of things in society, like avoiding motherhood and wanting individual recognition."

You also find fewer father-daughter combinations in the business world because it remains difficult for women to convince men to stop being chauvinistic or protective. Or, putting it another way, men are paternal to other men, but paternalistic to women.

To move into adulthood, first we must separate ourselves from our families at home and begin the long quest for our own identity without them. Can the sons and daughters of a corporate father stay his sons and daughters forever, or must they, too, eventually discard the role of child? Fathers fear this question and they realize that a father can keep his adult son around him much longer than his adult daughter. "Men can grow old, but women should not," flatly declared an executive who has worked with more than his share of beautiful young women.

Office fathers see sons as younger but different versions of themselves. Usually, they do not see daughters the same way. Daughters grow up, go away, get married, have babies. When they do not, the office father, like a natural father, feels confused and conflicted. He has no life script to prepare him for an aging daughter who stays on at work, and who someday may best him at the job, or, even worse, become his boss.

Fathers also fear rejection from daughters. They can kick out a son if he is disloyal, but the code of honor forbids most fathers from treating a woman that way. You just can't drop her "like a hot potato," the way one man described his dumping of disloyal employees.

Every man seeks a son "for a monument to the future," believes Dr. Mortimer Feinberg, a management consultant in New York City. Also, the man who seeks a son wants to leave a legacy to perpetuate his own beliefs, according to Dr. Mark Lipton, psychology professor at The New School in New York City, who told me, "A major point in wanting a son and needing a son is the question: Is there a son at home in the image of the father, or is he going to art school or ballet school?"

Dr. Feinberg has observed the same reaction. "I see a lot of men disappointed in their real sons. They don't meet the father's standards. He doesn't realize he's a freak in terms of energy, commitment, intelligence, drive. Yet the sons in business will often disappoint him as much as his own sons."

In addition to their doubts, anxieties, and disappointments over their natural sons, many executives feel guilty about their absence from home during the years they were building their careers—the early years when their children needed them the most. In late middle age, especially, they feel the loss of those years acutely. In order to stop feeling so guilty and lonely, they begin replacing the neglected son at home with a new son at work, thus proving that they *can* be a good father. In other words, they find "the child I never had, the child I always wanted."

"We know the father tries to be the kind of father he would have liked to be," Dr. Gerald Olivero, a psychologist and vice-president of the PA International management consulting firm in New York and Princeton, New Jersey, explained to me. "He tries to be a good father, better than his own father. He tries to find in the office son all the things he was or would like to have been. For example, the father may have determined that he was not a good supervisor of men. Now he wants his son to be a leader of men, and he creates that out of his own needs."

Many men are aware of this need to be better fathers than their own father, and better fathers than they were to their children, as I learned when I confronted them with the question.

"I wish I had had a real father," blurted out Sydney, a normally taciturn, inhibited man who owns a chain of men's clothing stores. "My father was a cop. He played my older brother off against me. He was never there when I needed him. I never knew if he was pleased with me or not."

A few days later, over a stringy, dry baked chicken on a jet bound for Chicago, I started a conversation with a gregarious automobile company division manager who described his father as a "brilliant engineer" but a disappointing parent. "My relationship with him was very competitive over my mother," Walter said. "I had a strong relationship with my mother, but contempt and disdain for my father. My only interest was in getting some recognition from him, and trying hard to get him to notice me."

Yet as fathers themselves at home, these men in the corporation were not as successful with their own children as they hoped they would be. "I can't make the same connections with my son and daughter because I don't know the specifics of their problems, the way I do with people in my office," Sydney had conceded.

Walter felt the same way. "I can't get as close to my two sons and daughter because I can't get as much information from them as swiftly or as authoritatively as I can in the office."

Fathers in the office were specific in explaining to me exactly what they are doing and why. They admitted the enormous ego satisfaction they felt—even the intimations of immortality—when they counseled their "sons." Several described a feeling of "seduction" (and that is exactly the word they used in separate conversations) in choosing their sons.

Fathering, they said, is an independent, self-taught trade, at times lonely, and usually publicly unrecognized and unrewarded. The corporation knows about it, benefits from it, but still never acknowledges it because that would probably be too heavy an emotional burden for both father and son to carry. Fathering may be the best-kept secret of American business today.

Who becomes a father and why?

Their personality traits are fairly predictable and remarkably similar.

In fact, Dr. Olivero of the PA International management consulting firm recognizes a father by a special pattern in the PA Preference Inventory (PAPI) value preference chart, a unique testing system developed to match the personality of the executive to the demands of the job. The pattern emerges on the chart from the answers to a questionnaire that tests management and organizational development. Dr. Olivero gives executives the test in order to counsel them on job moves, to find the root causes of their job conflicts, to help them understand job requirements, to realize how their own personality and values fit in, and to improve their management skills. The PAPI test chart is a profile of hidden personality characteristics that emerge when the executive chooses one of two responses to each of ninety questions. Answers to these questions reveal strengths and weaknesses for specific jobs.

Dr. Olivero finds that a profile of an office father shows a man with a great need to be in control of work and comfortable with leadership. He often serves as a consultant to his industry; he has a strong sense of entrepreneurship and is able to create his own business. He has great ability to analyze and weigh all the options; he is willing to discuss the possible consequences of his decisions; he is clear on alternatives, and he is savvy about company politics.

In what seems to be a contradiction, the father scores high on deference to authority but low on conformity. "That is common," Dr. Olivero reassured me. "Men like that break the rules and it doesn't matter."

The father, he explains, has a high need to get some support from authority and to give support to authority. Although he has learned all the rules in the organization, he knows which ones he needs to abide by and which ones he can safely ignore.

"The father knows how to break the rules," Dr. Olivero repeated for emphasis. "That is not rebelling. Basically, it's being creative, cutting time, getting things done more efficiently, and showing results earlier. He would try to teach the son how to cut corners in the corporation's social organization, as opposed to its formal organization."

For instance, senior executives may be asked to help younger staff pass professional certification examinations. The men who think of themselves as formal mentors play it straight down the line, giving only what they are supposed to give: specific coaching on the right answers in the test. But other men with different value systems will take a personal interest in their protégés, even going so far as to introduce them to the test examiner, saying, "I want you two to meet each other."

Now this might seem like an unfair advantage, Dr. Olivero said, but it is the way young men often get ahead. Instinctively I knew he was right. I had seen the process in action often enough.

As we analyzed fathers, he added another component of the father's personality which I found intriguing: Although fathers are men in control, they demand closeness and affection on the job—and they get it.

"My own office father, several years ago, may have become a father to me because he had a high emotional need to find somebody," Dr. Olivero recalled.

"He was nearing retirement. He thought that in me he had found the person he would leave to the organization. It's like insurance. You will have an impact after you are gone. If you hire this guy and train him, and he succeeds, they'll remember you and say, 'Hey, that's the guy who was trained by so-and-so.'

"It wasn't physical similarity that drew us together. It wasn't a common socioeconomic status. But it was genuine, free, social interaction in and out of the office. It was so easy for me to talk to him, and vice versa. He found comfort in me, as well as the other way around.

"Here's a guy sixty years old, in business, and he has learned some things as a result of being there and he has some theories of his own. So he talks about it with a youngster out of graduate school, and the youngster can document the older man's theories with research. He feels great. With my research, I've validated what he thought was true as a result of his experiences."

Today, Dr. Olivero has a son of his own at work. "I had a wide choice and I picked the best of the lot. I counsel him both generally and in terms of politics and of the job task.

"I really chose him before he chose me. It's unspoken, but he asked me specifically for my guidance. You don't take on a son, or 'mentee,' until you're fairly confident in your ability to win your own battles, until you stop fighting for yourself, and are able to give nurturing. He reinforces my own self-esteem. I'm always asking myself, 'What else can I teach him?' "

Next, I went to some other corporate fathers to ask them to talk about their "peculiar business," as one of them called the fathering process.

Chris, a fifty-two-year-old manager for a major computer firm in New York, closed the door to his paneled office, buzzed his secretary and asked her to hold his phone calls, and walked across his dove-gray carpet to gaze down from his thirty-second-floor window at the skaters below in Rockefeller Center.

"Why do I do this?" he asked in a frustrated growl. But I could tell he felt proud. "I like to tell myself that I want people to be there to replace me. I wish that I had had a father at work. I did have a protector, but not a father, not the way I am.

"A real office father is a natural adviser who takes pleasure in seeing people of talent not step into holes. Why do I do it? What do I get out of it? I don't know. Maybe some great big damned ego trip.

"The parental instinct never dies. When you're finished raising your own children, you've got some energy left over, so you're looking for someplace to put it.

"It occurs to you that you've gone through an awful lot, as a corporation person, learned a lot, had to invent your own wheel in many instances, cracked the secrets of the codes pretty much on your own, but sometimes with help. Freely given, gratuitous help. People who saw you struggling, took pity on you, and tipped you off.

"You look for the kind of person you are, the kind of mind set you've got. You're an abstract thinker or you're an intuitive thinker, and whatever you are, that's the kind of thinker you would look for. And you would show him how to make his contribution, as you had to learn how to make yours.

"The corporation is always taking on new people, and in a relatively small corporation or division of two hundred to two hundred fifty people, you get to see most of them, or you hear them in action at the various meetings. You get a notion of who is a striver, how much they've learned, what they've done to contribute, and what help they might need. Then you offer it, and if in the process, it gets accepted, and *you* don't get used, but *it* gets used—and there's a distinction— then somebody else has joined the clan.

"A son is someone who is struggling through things that you struggled through. And you want to make it easier for him, so he doesn't have to invent the damned wheel again. So you say, 'The wheel is here. Take it, Son. Take it, Daughter.'

"And furthermore, they are fully qualified for membership in whatever clan you may be developing in the corporation by their acceptance and understanding of what you're telling them. Fathers looking for corporate children can get rejected, and if they're smart, they don't offer themselves twice. There are too many needy ones out there. And you've got bread for them. If someone says, 'I don't want it,' you say, 'Screw you.' It's bad to throw the stuff away on the unappreciative. You don't want someone to grasp you around the legs and say, 'Thank you, thank you,' but you want it used.

"You don't dare mention the word 'fathering.' Scares the hell out of them. They may not see it that way. They may never think of you as their corporate father. They may never acknowledge you as more than a kindly fellow, passing out words of wisdom, but they will continue to qualify themselves by respectful attention to what you're telling them, and by putting it into practice. They've got to grow. Otherwise, you'd disown them."

I interrupted to remark that he was making it seem like pretty tricky business.

"It's really a question of hope and satisfaction in their progress," he replied. "It may very well be that that is the most emotion that will go into it. Sometimes it is inappropriate to put any more in it. And it might be rejected, especially if it is directed toward a younger woman. You've got to be damned careful about that one. 'Incest' may develop. That is a taboo. You have to be careful about how much raw emotion you allow. And you *can* control it.

"Once you've found your son or daughter, you don't lay down a general base and say things like, 'I'm your father and I'm going to guide you.' You just don't do that. But you might offer a helping hand on specific occasions. Now, if the advice is followed, and the result has been good, and the prospective son or daughter reports it back to you, what that amounts to is that the fish has taken the hook, and you do it just as delicately as an angler with a wary trap. Children are not easy to come by, in a corporate setting, or in the biological sense."

I wanted a specific example.

"Well, here's something, right out of today," he answered. "I said, 'Rick, our territory has been invaded by Art from the other division. He should not be here. However, Art has gotten so many rejections of his ideas in the last several weeks that we're not going to make an issue out of this. We are going to gently remind him that he stepped over the border. Will you take care of that for us? And remember, gently.'

"What the father is showing there is that just because someone has offended you—and turf stealing is a terrible offense—just because someone has done it, the shotgun blast is not always good. You try not to hit the wounded.

"Now Rick has learned a lesson. First of all, that turf is important. And second, that you don't shoot the wounded. I'll find out tomorrow if he picked up on the unspoken messages. I'll ask him if he took care of that little matter with Art. And I'll ask him what Art said. If that result was good, then we'll exchange a little satisfaction over that and go on again.

"I try not to get involved in Rick's personal life. I try to offer sympathy only. If you are asked for advice, and if you want to go to that level, you've got to exchange hostages. If you want something from him, you've got to give him something. He gives you an intimacy, you've got to give him one back. Otherwise, the conditions of friendship have been strained."

Chris swiveled his chair around and picked up that morning's newspaper, unfolded it, and glanced at the headlines. He began to reminisce.

"I started working on a newspaper when I was twenty-one, and I had sons even back then—copy boys and beginning reporters. When I learned something, I passed it on to them. In my late twenties and early thirties, I grew less tolerant, less sensitive, and that gradually reversed.

"I think it's related to the fact that I was learning my craft, growing professionally competent, and I needed every damn minute I had. Or, less self-servingly, I simply became mean and nasty, and wanted people to leave me alone. I needed less from above; therefore I gave less to below. Or maybe I had too goddamn much rivalry out there among the other reporters I was challenging from six other papers and the three wire services. . . . I know I certainly was not the greatest father to my own children during this time, working a trick that started at three in the afternoon and lasted until midnight. I never saw them.

"In my next job, I was hacking along as a staff writer with a trade organization and I had no sense that there were youngsters there trying to learn the same things I had learned ten years ago."

Chris was silent for a long time as the years tumbled by in his memory. "I didn't become a father again until I came here, where I had real authority. You seek out your sons or daughters, or they make themselves known to you. You make your offer, they accept it or reject it. If they accept, you start pouring it into them at appropriate times and at appropriate intensities, being real careful not to get the emotions started on these things.

"You take pleasure in their successes, you bleed with them over their failures, and you help them with their attitude, because attitude is all . . . not the altitude. The very young tend to see things in black and white. You give them some grays, some of the perspectives of their superiors, so they can see the issues their superiors are dealing with, so their superiors will start trusting them."

Then he turned to the subject of rebellion, and the way a father handles it.

"I think that someone who horsed off on his own against the good judgment of a corporate father and got his or her nose bloodied in the process would have to make the first step in coming back. In other words, the prodigal son would have to return. I wouldn't go out hunting for him.

"I don't think loyalty is the key issue here. Tractability is the issue: Can you continue to learn even though you might have rebelled? I've got to know whether or not this is the end of growth. The signal is: Do you have the damned good sense to come back and say, 'Hey, I made a mistake. Show me where I went wrong,' or 'Do me the favor of doing the same thing for me as you did before, when I didn't take your advice. I want the benefit of your advice again. I screwed up.'

"That is not a question of loyalty. That is a question of fulfilling, or refulfilling, the qualifications that made me a father in the first place. This is a teachable individual. You don't want to give the stuff away and have it wasted. It takes too long to get it right. And when it's wasted, or used against you, or you're betrayed, that is the end."

He grabbed a pencil and shook it at me to emphasize the point.

"If you're a son, you get one try at wasting. This is pure gold that we're talking about, that I'm ready to give away. This is the experience of a lifetime. Relevant, ready to use, right on the nubs. You can reject it once, but if you reject it twice, it's all over. The relationship is never the same. You're entitled to a mistake, but you are not entitled to be stupid.

"You can screw up once as a son. But you cannot betray. You cannot use information that was delivered freely to you to undercut the position of the person who gave it to you.

"That just happened to me. A guy wrote a memo over his name from advice I had given: 'Here's what we ought to do, here's how we ought to do it, here's when we ought to do it.' Using the hell out of my advice, and then taking credit for it. And he will never recover professionally. It's over for him. He will never again be able to use me or threaten me. He may go a little distance in this corporation, but it's going to be after I leave. I can block him. I can make it a him-or-me proposition, and it will be me. I will be able to do that on an issue basis; on a promotional basis, I won't because he is with our office in Chicago. But to the degree I can stop him, I will do it every time."

Corporate children cannot remain children for the rest of their careers. Fathers, too, must move on, through death, retirement, or job changes. Chris recognizes this.

"There comes a time when you have to cut them all loose, when you are doing things for them that they can do themselves with a little stretching. Or you're telling them things you've told them before that they should be able to figure out. Then it has reached a point where you're not a father, you're a crutch, and you've got to kick it out from underneath them. I've done it as ruthlessly as it can be done. Otherwise, they will always be sons, and you can't have it. That's not the way the world goes on.

"Sometimes the corporate offspring will be the one to end that relationship, saying, in effect, 'It's all over, Dad. I want more than you can show me. I've got to go on.' That signal comes when you offer some advice and they can improve on that advice. At that point, you speak sayonara. It's painful, but it is also very natural, and therefore must be accepted. When that happens, he or she flies better than you do, at least where they're going."

But it can be the other way, too, when a father must say the good-byes.

"Sometimes," Chris sighed, "you have to say, 'I'm not ready to leave this powerful place, and yet you are ready to assume it. You've got to go someplace else. There's no place in this nest for you.'"

Chris has seen too many young careers sidetracked after a father went out the door.

"When the father leaves for another job and maybe takes someone with him, or retires, the remaining sons are in mortal danger because the other 'families' in the organization who have made alliances elsewhere or are lower down on the scale are waiting for them. Usually, they should be able to anticipate this and try to find another corporate father."

Smart executives recognize the danger. "Lots of times, a man is not an overt corporate father. That's to protect his brood from attack lest he leave suddenly. Nobody else knows that he is protecting them and showing them the way around. When he disappears, the predators in the corporation will not know that this family is vulnerable. That's one reason a good corporate father does not go about bragging about how big a brood he's got. It makes them too vulnerable.''

By this time the weak winter sun was setting over the skaters and Chris was leaning back in his swivel chair, running his hands through his thin gray hair.

"Somebody's got to replace us. I've got an interest in the maintenance of society and culture. See, here's the real problem in life. A kid goes to college and learns how the Emperor of Rome lived. But he's never taught about the real world. And the kids who realize that swiftly look for protection when they get a job. We, the fathers, tell it because it's there to tell; there's no one else to tell it.

"It's utter chaos out there. Some people make things happen and organize the chaos. I don't know why I feel that obligation, but I do. I don't want to see people stumbling around in the dark, breaking the crockery—even though it's not my crockery."

He sat up straight, embarrassed at his intensity. "Every corporation knows in its heart of hearts that it will survive the bad people. No one person can destroy it. But they continue to make sure that no one can. I think the fathers in the corporation believe there is an interior body of knowledge to be learned. We're all interdependent. Nobody works alone these days. I feel a part of society.

"We need these new people before their energies burn out. The corporation leaves this to the father—the fathers without portfolio. It's almost a secret society we have.

"Sure, we select our sons. There's a bit of pride in that. We throw out the lure and see if the sons bite. Maybe they're not ready yet. But you throw out something and somebody recognizes it. You're always on the prowl for a son. When he comes to you, it's always a delight.''

Chris stood up. He looked restless, uncomfortable. Had he revealed too much? Just one more thought as he walked me to the door, a bit too swiftly, I felt. "Fathers tell their sons at work what the world is like. It's like driving a car. A good father doesn't let you lean on him too much. Sometimes you have to give a son a push. I view these young men as a younger version of me, and I'm constantly asking myself, 'Is he as good as I was?' ''

Unlike Chris, the next self-described father I interviewed had received at least informal industry recognition for his skill at fathering. They don't call it that, naturally. They call it "bringing so many good men along." Around Dallas, Jack, who is forty-nine, and heads a parts manufacturing division of a multimillion-dollar conglomerate, is famous for it.

Jack controls his division from a third-floor corner office in a sprawling concrete building in a suburban office park. He is a giant of a man, two hundred pounds, six feet two. His white laminated plastic desk looks as if he outgrew it a long time ago. Fortunately, he does not linger there. For like many successful managers, Jack hates sitting in the office. He is usually roaming the corridors, talking to his "boys." He is proud of his industry-wide reputation and that is the first thing he mentions to me.

"They say I have more vice-presidents here working for me than anyone else because they all started out as 'Jack's boys,' '' he boasted. "I'm considered to be the head of a whole brilliant school, and if I left, they would all follow me."

I asked him if the father chooses the son, or the son, the father.

"I think it's a bit of both. In each company, you find someone to hang on to. Nobody chooses a father who doesn't want the assignment. A young guy will say to me, 'Hey, Jack, I hope you will help me, work with me, because I'd like to steal from your experience.' And I'll say, 'Sure.'

"I pick up on personal traits. I like people who are hard-charging, who deliver a good day's work, people who are comers. Industry is so big that a man can't make it on his own. You are measured by your team. I don't see any one-man shows in history. But if you have all the boys with you, then top management has to listen to you.

"I have a father relationship to six or eight men at a time, and I have a unique reputation in the industry for this. That's how top people are picked. Otherwise, they don't have anyone to open doors for them.

"For example, I insist that my boys learn French and German because they'll be visiting foreign plants. I expose them to the social necessities of top management, too. In the office here, I'm very comfortable about what they wear. Even overalls and sandals don't bother me. But for meetings, I tell them to comb their hair and wear a suit. Otherwise, I won't let them make a presentation. I'll just say, 'I don't like the way you dressed.' It's sort of like, 'Hey, you want me to manage your career? Then don't embarrass me.' If you're moving successfully along, like I am, you can bring your people along."

He paused to take another swig of diet cola he always keeps on his desk. I asked him what qualities he looks for in a son. He put the can of cola down immediately. He liked that question.

"Persistence. Then loyalty to me. You know, two managers can look a guy over, and it's a form of seduction. They really seduce the guy, in a manner of speaking.

"And you don't share your children. I'm very jealous if I find my guy is working with someone else. I drop him like a hot potato.

"A guy has to pass a loyalty test with me. If they ask for advice and don't take it, I drop them. Do you want to spend your love and affection on someone who doesn't return it? I represent the local priest when it comes to my children. And, sure, I have a favorite. Most fathers would rank their children. The quality I want most is loyalty—that, and blind, unfailing trust."

One more thought, and he had to go to the second floor, to check on a new "son" who started work only two months ago. "You don't do this for the fun of it, but because it will help you. Maybe you do it in the sense of protecting yourself. And you know, everyone wants to leave something—best of all, some*one* well-taught, mature, politically aware. I hope they're better than I am and that they move into my position someday. But I don't know how I would react if I were working for one of my sons. That has never happened."

Their styles may be different, but Chris and Jack share the same convictions about corporate fatherhood and faith in the immortality it bestows. Chris and Jack represent the corporate father at his best, transmitting wisdom and experience to younger versions of themselves, leaving the corporations the best of themselves.

In conversations later on with other men, I began to hear about the other fathers—the ones who intimidate their "children," who abandon them, or who ultimately destroy them. Just like some natural fathers.

Corporate waters crawl with plenty of sharks and snakes, those older executives who destroy young men by dividing them, inciting them to fight among themselves for Daddy's attention and approval. Most often, I learned, this type of executive heaps both affection and insult on men who show him different faces of his own personality. It makes a fascinating case study—if you are not one of the victims.

George thrives on victims. George is a Boston truck driver's son who grew up to become president of one of the nation's top drug companies. He is the typical tyrant father, shouting, "Why in hell did you do it *that* way?" Or "Who told you that *you* had the authority to okay that shipment?"

When I became familiar with the routines in his office, I decided that George had three office sons, each representing a different side of himself.

Edward, the puckish Catholic intellectual, was the office court jester, unpredictable and unreliable, but charming, talented, and quite good at marketing, when he tried. Mainly, he liked to keep other people churned up. He would toss a chocolate bar on George's secretary's desk because he knew that Helen could never resist sweets. The next day, he would chide her with, "You really have to do something about those love handles, dear."

Leonard, a workaholic who directed the research for the company, was straight-and-narrow, a man George once described as being "too nice for his own good." Len was sophisticated, shy, serious, the only one that George could comfortably take to his favorite Chinese restaurant where they give you sugared walnuts instead of fortune cookies. Leonard wouldn't ask for any fortune cookies.

Phillip, the really bad one, most closely resembled the true George, rotgut off a tough Boston side street. Like George, Phillip was streetwise, crude, arrogant, impatient, and smart, a heavy drinker (especially when he was on the road selling the drugs to doctors) and a heavy womanizer. When he got into trouble with the police, George bailed him out and loved it, no matter how much he swore that this would be the last time.

These three men were rivals not only for George's affection, approval, and attention, but for the tangible proofs—better jobs, more money. George knew it and delighted in pitting one against the other. "Why can't you handle your department the way Leonard does?" he taunted Phillip. Or, "Leonard, I think that Phillip learned a long time ago that you've got to pace yourself at work and not try to do everything in one day." And, "Hey, Eddie, why is it that you're always wandering around the plant, never in your office the way Leonard is?" A typical office sibling rivalry pattern. One good child, two bad ones, locked in combat by the father.

"The setting of one son against the other—they do that all the time," Dr. Mortimer Feinberg, the management consultant, remarked impatiently when I described the situation.

"The person who wins in most cases is not the one who looks and acts like the father, but the one who opposes the father but does not let it go into open warfare," he said. "In other words, nobody wants a little sycophant. Everyone wants someone who is capable of being independent and, at the same time, sufficiently ingratiating so they don't go into open warfare.

"That's true up through the animal kingdom," Dr. Feinberg continued. "The monkey that gets into perpetuity, which means that it gets its sperm into a female, is the one who doesn't anger the head monkey. The one who angers the head monkey by challenging him too often never gets around to getting his sperm into anything."

In each office, sons will be rivals for the father's position. "The father's fear is that the sons will replace him eventually, which of course they will," said Dr. Feinberg. "The father wants his sons to be successful, but not so successful that it makes his success seem easy. At the same time, he has pride, so there is a great deal of ambivalence.

"Fathers demand blind, unswerving loyalty. Their sons must follow the rules. As long as they do what the father tells them to do, when he wants them to do it, they will get money and a lifetime kind of commitment."

In Dr. Feinberg's opinion, the Japanese are much better at all this than Americans, and we might well emulate them. Japanese corporations bring retired executives back to guide young people on the way up, thereby eliminating much of the power struggle among the sons for the father, and eliminating the father's fear and ambivalence as well.

That is not likely to happen here. Instead, Dr. Feinberg predicts more Big Daddies for American firms. "In times of crisis, you're going to have father figures emerging. American industry is in very bad shape now—steel, automobiles, housing, retail. So you will see more men like Bill Paley, the autocratic old father, who is now finished with searching for a son."

In the corporate world a legendary strict father was Harold Geneen, president of ITT. One former employee remembers that Geneen proclaimed, "I motivate by intimidation," and because he did, turnover was high at ITT. Yet certain types of people thrived in that atmosphere.

Geneen's opposite in management style was Irving Shapiro, chairman and chief executive of E.I. du Pont de Nemours & Co., Inc. If a corporate, symbolic father could also be a nurturing parent (and this may well be the father of the future) he was seen that way because of his concern about "motherly issues" like environmental protection.

Fathers like Mr. Shapiro, Mr. Geneen, and Mr. Paley are so completely identified with their companies that it is impossible to think of one without the other. How does this affect the employees of the corporation? Are they better off with a high-visibility father than with a what's-his-name—better off with Frank Borman of United Airlines than with ? of American Airlines; with Lee Iacocca of Chrysler than with ? of Chevrolet?

The fame of a corporate father cuts two ways, cautioned Dr. Harvey Barocas, Baruch College psychology professor, in our conversation. Depending on the quality of interaction between a corporate father and his family, his fame can promote individual growth in employees or it can intimidate them. However, very often famous corporate fathers do serve as important role models in the company.

All fathers are role models to their natural sons and to their office sons. The natural sons carry on the father's name. The office sons carry on his work. In the office son, the son he chooses, a father truly leaves his legacy—the best of himself—to run the company.

If this seems cruel, arbitrary, and a violation of the principle of hard work and talent bringing their own rewards, so it is. The corporation has little use for people who just work steadily but have neither the stomach for office politics nor the personality to attract a mentor.

"The corporation is right to expect that if someone is going to move up, that someone will very quickly make himself or herself known," says Robert Waldron, director of the New York media office of the American Council of Life Insurance and the Health Insurance Association of America in Washington, who has analyzed the power scene for a long time, and who himself is a corporate father.

Those people who decide to move up, he told me, will get on a fast track, and know where that track is. "They will attract all of the help that comes from mentors, who are looking for people with brains and skills and guts and persistence, people willing to pay all kinds of prices.

"The corporation is right not to look for 'growth' in people, because 85 percent of them never move," he said. "There is one place in the corporation for them—where they started. They're never going to go any further. They may rise to manager of their department by slow degrees by the time they're sixty, and get the gold watch. But that's where they are going to stay and they're not going to be recognized. You have to knock on those doors and ask for what the fathers can give."

Bob Waldron feels that we are in the midst of a crisis in corporate leadership. "If the world needs anything, it needs sensitive people who think oceanically, who have a little more of the Renaissance man about them than the specialists we're turning out, who can see other people's point of view. The world needs transactors who can act between the various specialties that separate people. The world needs leaders with some guts, and some sensitivities to discover what a goal is, where we ought to be going, and the persistence to pick up the leadership qualities that are necessary to get us there. It used to be that the world would train its leaders. Now they select themselves. And finding a father is one way they do it."

Leadership. To Bob Waldron and to other corporate executives, that is a do-it-yourself project, a contract made by few older men who want, more than anything else, to leave a legacy to the young who want, more than anything else, to move up fast.

Fathers. No executive reaches the top, or comes anywhere near it, without them. But for every father, there must be a son. Or several sons.

THREE

The Son:
Heir Apparent

"The sons want to fulfill the expectations of the father, whatever they perceive the father to want."
—DR. SAMUEL SQUIRES, *psychologist and management consultant*

If I had been born a boy, would my father have left? I have always wondered about that. It is a question impossible to answer, painful to contemplate, and one I ask only rarely, late at night, under the blankets. The inner voice that comes back to me whispers, "He might not have gone, not so soon. Maybe he would have stayed only a little bit longer, but, then, maybe a lot longer." So I have for years assumed that if I had been his son and not his daughter, our lives would have changed and we would have been together. At least for a while.

Yet, in desiring a son, he was no different from nearly all men—and women, too—who want a boy, first and most. It has always been so. Down through the ages, a son has been a universal promise of immortality, a joyous, crowning achievement, proof of a father's masculinity and, inexplicably, a mother's femininity.

Sons are equally treasured in the corporate family. The son is the second most important person in the corporate family—next to the father, whom he may eventually replace.

Most young men entering the corporation seem to know this instinctively, as they jockey for the attention of older executives, hoping to become the favorite of one or two. I have noticed that young men who do not realize this or refuse to accept it find their careers sidetracked or slow-tracked. (In a similar way, a natural son, shy, angry, or frustrated, may refuse to engage his father's interest and may be pushed to the sidelines at home, his desires ignored so his father can accommodate the demands of a brighter, more aggressive son or daughter.)

Not all men are corporate sons. But almost all young men are potential sons. For them, beginning a career can mean a second chance at sonhood, at becoming a favorite with a corporate father if they failed in a relationship with a real one. In a new corporate family, a young man starts with a clean slate. He can look around, assess the scene, and decide which man best suits his personality. Sometimes it's just luck when a son gets a corporate father and sometimes it's the deliberate selection of one or both. Most of the experts I met believed that it was not so much chance as choice.

A cool late-August rain had misted the green hills and white fences of the horse country in Pound Ridge, New York. I drove down a side road to a triangle-shaped modern house designed and built (with hammer-and-nail construction assistance from friends) by Dr. Samuel Squires, psychologist, management consultant, president of Interactive Testing and Training Systems, Inc. and Personnel Management Systems of Larchmont, New York. A week before, I had learned from friends that he held some spirited and unorthodox opinions about corporations and corporate people. I was not to be disappointed that night.

As we sat on the brown suede sofa that curled halfway around the living room, and talked of families at work, I asked him first if a young man could ever succeed without a father. He shook his head. "I would probably say, 'No,' for a lot of reasons."

There were the obvious ones, of course. The ambitious young, if they are to rise above their peers, need the wisdom, the experience, the guidance, the personal attention of those already in power. But Dr. Squires also saw it from another angle. The company, he said, would lose its most innovative people were it not for the older executive who reaches out to the misfit.

"A father in the corporation is probably the only one who will accept the 'butch,' the bad child, who marches to a different drummer," Dr. Squires commented. "The father can accept and love that child not only for who he is, but for who he is not. He doesn't quite fit in, but you accept him and love him, and you don't fire him. You accept his ideas. But were you not his corporate parent, you would call him just a precocious kid and you would fire him."

Dr. Squires is a man who likes mavericks, perhaps even (or especially?) when they are obnoxious, and he identifies with risk takers who are full of creativity, persistence, and the courage of their convictions. Without the protection of an older man, he believes, these men could never find their way into upper management. Even middle management.

How, I asked, does a young man, especially a maverick, or a "nut," ever find a father? Or does the father find the son first?

It's probably a little of both, Dr. Squires thought. "Invariably, there is a need. Or people like people who are images of themselves. Or you have an older person who identifies with a younger person, and vice versa.

"Maybe the younger person is more exploitive, using the older one to get ahead, yet they both use each other. The older person is probably satisfying a personal need, not a professional need."

To a second expert it was, first and foremost, the similarity of physical characteristics that drew the older man and the younger one together. Dr. Gerald Olivero, psychologist and vice-president of the PA International management consultant firm, said that those two destined for a closer office relationship react to each other with a feeling of "You look like me . . . I'm going to talk to you." After that, Dr. Olivero assured me, socioeconomic status becomes an important factor in strengthening the bond between them. For instance, this type of reasoning may run through an executive's mind as he interviews a job applicant: "Well, we understand each other. I see from your résumé that your father was a doctor. My father was a doctor, too."

The father-son office relationship is a symbiotic one, each man providing what the other lacks, Dr. Olivero went on. For example, the father has a low need to finish tasks; the son, a high need.

Yet in many ways, they are alike. Both have forceful and open personalities, work hard, have a high need to achieve, feel comfortable as leaders, and need change in their lives and in their careers. Both want to control other people as well as the work flow under them.

In addition, the son needs to feel responsible for the time and commitment he gets from the father, and must demonstrate that feeling by his loyalty, deference, affection, and endearments. "He is responsible for making sure the father feels okay," said Dr. Olivero. "It is not enough just to perform well."

One way a son shows "endearments" to a father is by inviting him to a health club, because, as Dr. Olivero noted, "Just the fact that you would *consider* exercising with somebody your senior makes him feel good!"

The son must also thank the father for his time and, even more urgent, convey to him the message "I respect you. You're important to me and my job. I don't know what I'd do without you. You're great; you're wise."

Now that I understood a few of the psychological aspects of the "office-son" relationship, it was time to talk to some of the rising stars in various corporations.

As young men discussed the problems of "making it," I was struck by their candor in admitting that they were consciously adopting the manner of a son, or grateful subordinate. I was amazed by their acknowledgment of manipulation of the older men. Then I was saddened by a certain sense of desperation I detected in some of the conversations as the men revealed their feelings.

First of all, the junior executives agreed, similarities in personality and physical traits were critical in helping them win over an older man.

For Vince, it was the Midwest connection. Starting out as a copy boy on the Cleveland *Press,* Vince worked his way up to reporter, then bounced in and out of small local TV stations in Cleveland, Indianapolis, and Pittsburgh before he got his big break writing the morning news for the network's flagship station in Chicago.

"I had a lot of things to learn all at once," he told me. "I lucked into working for this incredible man, a giant in the industry, who heard my Midwest pronunciation of the word 'water' one day—the word that gives away your origins faster than any other. He came over and talked to me, and it turned out that he had gone to the University of Ohio, too, and covered politics for the Cleveland *Press* years ago. From that day on, he took a special interest in me.

"I was the one person he could really mold and build, because my writing had a style that other people's didn't. He needed me, he decided, to hype the programs and boost the ratings by coming up with scripts for quick investigative stories for the on-air talent. Early on, I realized that was exactly why he had hired me, because I wrote the way he couldn't. I could be witty or ironic or poignant or be a bastard going after city hall, and I could bring a thousand words down to one paragraph. He could never do any of that. Because I could, and, I guess, because I talked the way he talked, he took me under his wing. At the same time, he fed me with a lot of things that I needed to know, coming into a big network operation from small stations.

"He was concerned about my income, about my welfare, about how I behaved in the political sense. The biggest thing had to do with dress codes. I was coming out of the boondocks, and all I owned were corduroy jackets. One afternoon we were supposed to meet the new network vice-president and some local affiliate managers about the possibility of expanding our newscasts. I was wearing a brown cord jacket and a yellow golf shirt with chinos. He took me aside, handed me his blue blazer, which luckily wasn't too big on me, and told me to buy a white shirt and striped tie at lunch. 'Dress every day as if you are going to an important meeting,' he said."

After two years Vince was promoted to a writer's job on the evening newscast. "There I ran into what I call the 'phony father.' This is a guy—we've all seen people like him—who loves to be Mr. Big Cheese, to say, 'I'll help you, show you around, take you to lunch,' and all that, but he does absolutely nothing for you. He forgets your raise, he forgets the memo you sent him last week, he forgets the plans for the convention next month, he forgets everything except that he has to leave at four for his squash game. But he loves to feel like your father. I had to learn to 'massage' him, just to survive, because he could get me taken off the show. I had to do my job and part of his.

"When he first took over the show, he had an executive assistant whom he promoted and who became his real son. Three months later, that guy was promoted to manager. He wasn't ready for it because he didn't know how to handle either the off-camera creative people or the talent. In the business we were in, that eventually slides you out.

"But he was absolutely Ted's favorite and that was that. Ted had apparently relied on him so heavily when he first took over the job that this guy had given his blood for Ted. Well, Ted wasn't about to forget that and he made up his mind to protect this guy at any cost. I think there is more to it than that, though. I think a bond was somehow made, maybe the kind of bond I made with Don when I came into the company. People make those pattern bonds and stick to them. They last because they relate to good experiences in a person's life, and they make a pattern in the mind which is very hard to change."

After leaving Vince, I called to make an appointment with Bradley, whom I had met earlier at a journalism and law seminar. We had both arrived early, and as we talked about our jobs, he had mentioned the necessity for playing games at work. I was curious to find out exactly what he meant.

Bradley is short, flabby-plump, with a grin that masks his anxiety about finishing his probationary year in a high-powered law firm and his eagerness to join the firm permanently. He has a wife and three-month-old daughter at home in a $975-a-month apartment.

At twenty-eight he is two years out of an Ivy League law school and considers himself lucky to be one of the 180 lawyers in one of the nation's largest and most prestigious firms. He is scared, but he is smart. He is also having a hard time finding his "father."

"People around me, at my level, definitely know the game they are playing," he told me bluntly. "And since the ones on top got there by playing the same game, I'm sure they know, too.

"The game is so accepted that you don't think of it as a game, but as a part of life here, and there are many different ways of playing."

Over wonton soup in a no-nonsense Chinatown restaurant with glass squares covering plastic tablecloths, Brad recited the first rule as if he had memorized it long ago: "You really won't make it unless there are a significant number of older people who will push your cause. If you're quiet and hang in the background, you'll get lost in the shuffle. If you're a drone, putting out quality work, with no relationship to an older man, you're just not going to make it at all.

"As a political matter, you know which of the sixty partners carries the most weight. Like, one day, a partner took an interest in me, asking about my new daughter, and I said to myself, 'This is not doing me a lot of good. I'd do better to be friendly with the heavyweights.'

"So I managed to get the office next to one of them, to get into his orbit. If he had his eye out for you, you had it made. You've got to read his personality and play into it. He's an egomaniac. Nice guy, but he'll tell you one of his accomplishments any chance he gets. And you'd better be ready to listen and applaud. He eats that stuff up.

"He loves practical jokes, too, so I bought a book of them. To make it with that guy, you've got to play jokes, tell jokes, play his game, *and* do the kind of work he likes."

Brad finished the soup and picked up his chopsticks to dig into the chicken and cashew nuts. "You have to tailor your work to the litigating style of any partner you're working for," he continued. "But it's not that hard to do. For the quiet one, you would write in your legal brief that the plaintiff's lawsuit 'lacks merit.' For the flamboyant one, you would write, 'My opponent's scurrilous action is meant solely to harass and for the purpose of dragging my name through the mud.'

"Younger lawyers like me do all the dirty work—the phone calls, the research. The partner will mainly have the contact with the clients and will come into the courtroom to try the case. The partner will call me into his office to find out where the case is, to see how to bill the client.

"You inevitably do more work for some people and it helps if you have one or two men to push you. But you've got to stay buddy-buddy with as many people as possible. You must do good work and you must look presentable, and that means carrying yourself as an attorney should.

"You have to wear a suit, but you don't have to wear just white shirts. They can be yellow or even striped. Of course, our firm is Jewish, and there are some significant distinctions between Jewish firms and WASP firms. Jewish firms are looser in terms of clothing. Also, you can walk into most partners' offices, and the partners are much more approachable. I worked as a clerk and as a paralegal at a WASP firm before I came here. At the WASP firm, there was a lot less emphasis on relationships.

"Here, they want their work environment to be as pleasant as possible. The partners love for people to flatter them. They are big talkers, and love to be told how wonderful they are. But a lot of the stories are interesting, and you're happy they are willing to talk with you. A lot of people won't waste their time talking to you."

After a year of searching, Brad found a man to take a special interest in him, a younger partner in the firm, only thirty years old, and, like Brad, short and chubby.

"We first got to know each other because we're both Met fans and most of the guys here are Yankee fans. Sometimes we would talk baseball for an hour at a time in the mornings. Then we began having lunch together, and he got to know me and like me, and he would tell me how to write up the briefs to please the different partners, and how important it was to wear Brooks Brothers suits. I feel very friendly with him, not competitive at all, although that might change the longer I stay with the firm and get closer to making partner myself.

"In my own head, I think about how I am doing; whether I command as much respect as I should, whether I am getting as good work as the others, whether I am doing as good work as others. I need this older man to tell me I am doing a good job, which is exactly what I need—yes, still need—from my own father. To this day, I still eat it up, when he praises me for getting a good job, for having a nice child, for leading a good life."

A few months ago Brad learned the most valuable lesson of his young career from the man he is so carefully cultivating.

"Our firm's team was supposed to play a baseball game and I was first baseman. At five-thirty, just as I'm getting ready to walk out the door, he calls me with a little research assignment for a court case. Now, usually, he's a reasonable guy and I can talk to him, so I said, 'Let's put this off until tomorrow. I want to go play baseball tonight.'

"Well, he just blew up. He went through the roof, called me 'irresponsible,' yelled at me that I was 'just a kid.' I was stunned and hurt. The next day I confronted him and told him all that was bullshit.

" 'You can't talk to me that way,' he said. 'By virtue of the fact that I was born ten years before you were, I control your fate in this office.' "

Brad was furious, but once his anger subsided he realized that he had acquired valuable experience from this encounter with the older partner. "He was willing to say that to me because he cared about me, because he really is like a father to me. So I have learned that if I want to stay in this law firm, I have to be very careful what I say to whom, even to him."

Early in his legal career, Brad has figured out the fundamental rule of corporate life: To succeed, a young man needs an older one (or several) to pull him up, and to succeed big, a young man needs to become not just a good son, but a favorite son, to a man who will take more than a coolly professional interest in him. A young man must also know how to keep the relationship intact, to push the buttons that preserve the rapport between the two of them. Even if it takes a bit of manipulation.

Unlike Brad, who has a comfortable relationship with his real father, Douglas, who works in an investment firm, failed to learn the son's game for survival and success at work. He has finally figured out why. He never knew his real father. Out of that deprivation emerged a continuing search for a father wherever he worked. I knew how he felt.

"My father owned a grocery store and worked all the time, seven days and nights every week," Douglas said. "While I was growing up, I had no concept of a father, or of an appropriate male image. And it is still not there. It is a gap, a blank in my neurological system and psychological experience. I have spent most of my life trying to fill that gap.

"First I tried to fill it with Lloyd, who was maybe not so much father to me as older brother, or maybe just the adult, positive male identity that I wanted to emulate. He embodied in many ways the kind of political and academic man of the world that I wanted to become.

"Basically, he tried to manipulate me. He knew I wanted approval, and he pushed the approval button a great many times in many ways. And I was too young and dumb to understand that winning his approval would not result in an objective merit judgment that would get me more money or more power.

"All I kept getting were these temporary approval shots. Lloyd had a problem with our boss, Frank, who ran the entire operation. He was always trying to get his approval. I wanted to be Frank's son, too. He was one of that small group of demigods in the firm, people of extraordinary brilliance and decency. If there is a father element in my relationship with him, it is because he paid attention to me. He was present. Never absent. He recognized me at my best and did not discount that from my worst. He was loyal and he was there—all the time, and that's a lot.

"We were all in competition in that office for money, power, rank, and job security. I don't think that Frank set us up to fight with each other. It just worked out that way. He believed that the conflict among colleagues in the search for truth should be like that in a college community."

But when the conflict erupted among those colleagues, and when the young men surrounding him challenged him, how did Frank react? Douglas's answer was eloquent testimony to the fear of loss. "My gut reaction is that I was too scared of him to challenge him. Anyway, I was beginning to be ostracized. I kept trying to get into the group and failed. That used to bother me, but gradually it stopped. I realized that the need to get into the 'in' group, the surrogate family, was a very neurotic need in me."

Douglas wanted to become a favorite son, but could not even get into the family circle. Brad, on the other hand, has schemed and plotted to get his office close to the legal firm's partner who can do him the most good. Vince, luckiest of the three, had the good fortune to fall into a comfortable role immediately with his boss at the Chicago TV station.

The favorite son in the office, according to management consultant Dr. Mortimer Feinberg, feels two conflicting emotions—hostility and love—for his corporate father and must "kill" him, or surpass him, to some degree in order to establish his own identity.

"The favorite son becomes the person who wants to kill the father," Dr. Feinberg emphasized during our conversation. "Abraham's son was Isaac, and Isaac destroyed his father's inventory of idols. In each office the sons will be rivals for the father, and the father's fear is that the sons will replace him eventually, which, of course, they will."

Dr. Squires tended to see the favorite child in a more benign light. The favorite child, he told me, is the favorite child no matter what he does, simply because the father has such strong feelings about him. The father can identify with this son, and project his own feelings onto him easily.

"He allows him to enter into him," Dr. Squires said. "It's fulfillment, it's ego, it's 'I am responsible for you,' it's a whole lot of psychological mechanisms.

"We human beings," he continued, "make decisions based on our feelings, not our intellect. Once we have a feeling identified, we will find all the intellectual reasons to rationalize it, to justify how we feel. We'll find all the evidence. It's like knowing statistics. You can make anything come out the way you want."

Because they have such status in the organization, young men who are singled out as special begin to change the nature of the organization itself. Their values and attitudes, their dress and their manners become the standards by which all else is judged.

Here's one example of how it works in newspaper offices: A new managing editor fires the old city editor, who had been originally hired by his predecessor. He promotes his own man to that critical slot.

Almost immediately, under the Young Turk, feature stories begin to appear with soft leads and longer paragraphs. Wearing blue jeans around the city desk is suddenly accepted when before it used to draw comments such as "You just coming in from the barn?" Public relations account executives are stopped at the receptionist's desk when only yesterday they were hand-delivering their press releases into the newsroom.

Major changes like these are inevitable when a new boss appears. Only the specifics are different in each business.

As the most powerful person on his immediate turf, the favorite son produces a boomerang effect on the people around him, especially those who used to be his equals, his "brothers" and "sisters." For to get where he is, he had to beat someone else out. Once there, he can bully, tyrannize, encourage, or promote—but he does not remain neutral. Too much is at stake. Usually, he quickly becomes a kind of father himself, although not taken very seriously at first, until he hires new people. When he picks his own special favorites, inevitably he sets them in competition with each other.

Sibling rivalry is built into the fabric of the American corporation, and nobody has to deliberately set young men against each other, according to Dr. Squires, who clearly hates the whole idea.

"The sons want to fulfill the expectations of the father, whatever they perceive the father to want," he commented tersely. "That's internalized. Whether or not it is stated overtly by the father is not important. Because of our personal family relationships, it isn't necessary to state it. We are so conditioned to hear our father say, 'You must get A's in school,' or 'You must succeed,' that it is no longer necessary to be conditioned to achieve, or to get ahead within the company—in spite of the fact that it might make you unhappy."

He frowned and gazed out the picture window, his face registering distaste and, at the same time, resignation. "It's something crazy about American people that you might have a chemist working at a bench, working very happily, and doing terrific work as a chemist, coming up with better formulas all the time. Then one day his boss announces that there's an opening for supervisor of the lab. The chemist, of course, applies for it, and gets it, beating out a couple of others to do so. Now, somebody who has been perfectly happy as a chemist becomes a supervisor because he thinks he ought to. He hates it, and he's not very good at it, but he feels he has to stay for the status, the recognition, the prestige. And this happens all the time, in all kinds of industries."

Yes, sibling rivalry may be built into the structure of the corporation, but it is deeply resented by some who are forced into cutthroat competition, as I learned from a senior vice-president for a moving and storage company. "At first, I refused to participate, but then I got sucked into it," admitted Ernie. "What's funny is that I, who considered myself a noncompetitor, was perceived by everybody around me as being an archcompetitor. I didn't want anything to do with that jazz. I kept on going my own way. But in doing that, when I was sales manager at the time, I kept doing things that were intensely visible, without even realizing it. People resented it and began to compete with me.

"I had no choice. I was forced—we were all forced—into this situation by a man who set us at each other's throats by yelling, 'You *will* work together!' Where I had been able in the past to get everything I wanted by making deals, suddenly nobody wanted to deal because we were all in competition with each other.

"It's a terrific motivation factor, you see. There are two ways to get people to do things for you. One is to make everyone compete against each other and force them all to outdo each other to achieve productivity. The other way is just to motivate people in positive ways by rewarding them. This vice-president succeeded in keeping people divided and all loyal to him because they didn't have much time to do anything else. We were all distrustful of each other, alienated, all competing for a crumb of praise that would be gone the next day. It was a terror situation: 'You *will* do.' We all knew what we had to do. That we had better do it. And we did."

Well, I argued, it certainly worked.

Ernie bristled. "This kind of thing works short-term, but in the long term, it doesn't work like building relationships within a department.

When the year was up and the job this vice-president was pushing for came up, he didn't get it. Everybody at the top had been watching the whole game and they got scared the more they saw his behavior with us. He was transferred to a smaller department.''

Then a new boss took over. The sons had to start all over again. Potentially, a great advantage for them.

According to the management consultants (and most people's office experience confirms this) the departing father's favorite son rarely becomes the favorite of the new boss. But a young man who has toiled on the fringes, relatively unnoticed, stands a good chance of becoming the favorite—unless the new boss brings in his own or hires one from the outside.

However, during the transition period, the office is in turmoil and morale sinks to a new low. "The rumor mill starts up," said Dr. Squires, "and so does the back-stabbing. You don't know whom to trust anymore. You're not sure whether you have told your friend down the hall too many things."

Ambitious young men keep busy feeding their new boss with ideas, information, and gossip. Trying to learn all he can as fast as he can about the staff and their strengths and weaknesses, the new boss will often encourage them with the invitation "Come on out and have a beer with me after work and we'll talk."

But beware of the potential damage you may do to your career, warned several people who regretted accepting that invitation. Letting your hair down with the boss makes you more vulnerable to his evaluation of your personality than your ability. Be cautious and not totally candid. Remember, you're still at work—even over a beer at the bar— and he's still sizing you up. (Yet occasionally going out for a casual meeting off the office grounds can work to your advantage—if you play it right and never forget that the odds favor your boss.)

"During that year of reorganization," continued Dr. Squires, "brother is stabbing brother, going in and having little private conferences with the new father, and acting as sophisticated as possible, but actually trying to cut off somebody else's legs in order to appear taller."

After the new boss finally gets the lay of the land and the staff sorted out, he starts the bloodbath, as Henry, the editor with the daughters, did with us on that suburban newspaper. "Somebody has to be the sacrificial lamb, the scapegoat," pointed out Dr. Squires. "The new person establishes his authority by firing, transferring, hiring, promoting, or shoving some people aside."

By that time it is clear who the new sons are going to be because they assume the more responsible positions in the office. The favorite sons of the old father have now become the stepchildren. At the end of a year, the office is completely reorganized with the new boss, who usually justifies his changes by declaring that the company benefits from his streamlined style of administration.

Inevitably, some people refuse to become intwined in these relationships. Dr. Squires described them as the "noninvolved ones who generally are not empire builders, who just go on and do their jobs no matter who is the boss, because it doesn't make any difference to them."

They will never be considered as candidates for better jobs. But they won't get fired, either. That's the trade-off.

"For the most part," said Dr. Squires, "these people are direct and keenly aware of what they are doing. They will be able to verbalize it: 'I am not involved. I don't want anyone to be my "father" at work. I am just going to do my job. Period.' "

Then there are the men who have rejected the role of son after needing it for so long. I thought of Sam, an old friend who heads the claims department of an insurance company. When I visited him early one morning in an office building near mine, he was already deep into a blue folder, one of six stacked on his mahogany desk. Sam closed the folder, ordered us coffee, and sat back, hands behind his head, recalling a long work history of emotional involvement with his bosses, especially one in particular. "Many times, I tried to make Arnold into an older brother, or father, because he was the most extraordinary, brilliant, incisive, witty person I ever met. But he wasn't interested in being my father. He deflected it, and helped me get perspective by not responding. As a result, we had an incredibly productive working relationship."

Sam rubbed the back of his neck and waited a couple of minutes before he spoke again. "Maybe it's because I'm getting older and people are starting to turn to me like I'm their father. But when my radar begins to pick this up, I walk away from it. I think a lot of the son-father business is unhealthy.

"I feel that I have grown out of, well almost completely out of, that kind of neurotic acting out with family surrogates that I engaged in when an older man said, in effect, 'I will give you a career, a life, a direction, if you will follow me,' and I replied, in my head, 'I will do anything for your approval and love.' I was really in a juvenile and adolescent phase of my life in my earlier jobs. Eventually, I guess, I quit my last job because my boss and I both wanted to be the special person, or the favorite, if you will, to the president of the company.

"The male problem," Sam concluded, his voice rising, "is that all the sons are aware that they are rivals. Sure, you can be friends, but it's usually got an edge to it. Now I know that you can refuse the role of son, and father, too, by developing a clear sense of your own identity and worth."

But, as Bob Waldron said, the ones who want to play the game make themselves visible. These are the young men who see themselves as sons, as risk takers, as major political players in an organization. They either stay in the game or get shut out of it at certain times, depending on circumstances. But what sets them apart from the others is their recognition of the need to play the game if they want to go up.

A man never has to stop being a son, even if he is a father himself. In fact, knowing when you need a father is a critical step in the advancement of a career, as well as its development.

For fifteen years Craig had headed up the Little Rock sales office of a furniture manufacturing firm, reporting to the manager of the New Orleans regional headquarters. Suddenly, in a takeover by the new board of directors against the old-timers, the manager for the past twenty years was fired, and Craig was summoned to take over the New Orleans headquarters. Craig realized that he had little feel for the day-to-day politics of headquarters operations, and he did not know much about the people there because he had been in Arkansas so long.

So, naturally, once he was settled in the blue-carpeted office with the original paintings of Bourbon Street back in the 1900s, he looked around for help. He found it in Charles, his second-in-command, a man considerably older, who knew who was who and where the bodies were buried. Although Craig was Charles's boss, Craig cultivated Charles because he knew he needed him, and the two spent many hours in closed-door conferences and two-hour lunches. "He protected my ass and showed me the ropes," Craig told a few close friends.

Charles, of course, was Craig's temporary father, serving a useful if limited purpose. His real office father, who had promoted him through the years and sent him to head the Little Rock office, was the manager dismissed in the coup. This happens frequently in the corporate world.

How much better for all concerned for an executive to be dismissed or transferred than to stay on and work as a subordinate under those he once supervised!

I remember Harvey, a man with a long and distinguished career in the engineering world, who was demoted as vice-president. In the opinion of the company president, Harvey had become too "picky," demanding that the junior members of the firm rework the specifications for so many jobs. Harvey was "asked" (ordered) to accept a newly created position of "associate director" reporting to Gordon, a young man he had hired only two years before. At first Harvey thought he could handle it, and worked a year and a half as an equal to staff members whose drawings he once criticized and sent back for revisions. Eventually the humiliation was too much to bear, and he finally found another job with a smaller firm.

"There is, of course, a great deal of resentment on the part of the original father in situations like this," Dr. Squires declared, again with regret. "It takes an unusual person to be able to wish the son a lot of luck when he has surpassed the father and has a superior position. There are a lot of ambivalent feelings and a lot of anger and hostility, which very few people will acknowledge. They will just try to rationalize it by saying that the son was promoted for another reason."

Sometimes the office father is passed over and the son he trained is promoted because the father does not have the personality to get along with people. The older man will be considered too direct, or blatant, or aloof, or too much a know-it-all.

After sons become their father's bosses, the relationship becomes the son's responsibility—although few handle it well. When Dr. Squires counsels executives about this situation, he recommends that both men acknowledge the "dignity and the integrity" of the older man and his contributions to the company.

The worst situation of all is the dilemma of the unwitting and un-willing son—picked out and picked on by an older man with neurotic, near-sadistic impulses. Recall, in the preceding chapter, the story of George, who had three office sons.

George related to each man in a different way because he needed to be a father in different ways to accommodate different aspects of his personality. He found, or else he created, three victims—one serving his warped sense of humor, one his vanity, and another his insecurity.

On a newspaper some years ago an editor I will call Tim decided that a new reporter I will call Mike was the "office bastard"—yes, that's exactly what he told us all. Jokingly, of course. But actions be-lied the joking words. Tim was always out "to show Mike a thing or two"—which usually amounted to the equivalent of a public hanging. "Can't you people from California ever learn to spell?" he would yell across the crowded city room as he threw the copy paper at Mike's typewriter. Or, he would shout, "How many times do I have to tell you that on this paper we don't capitalize anything except President! And that's President of the United States, and nobody else, dummy!"

Through it all, Mike told us he really didn't care, that everybody knew Tim was a nut anyway, so to hell with him. But Mike did care. He was hospitalized for a bleeding ulcer after a couple of years and eventually developed a drinking problem. Then he married and moved to his wife's home town. I never saw him again, but I often think of him and I wonder what we would have been like, and what our paper would have been like, had we not been so caught up in the craziness of one editor. He affected us all. I tried to get my days off changed to the days when Tim was working, so I would only have to endure him for three days. So did other reporters. Coming in on

Saturdays and Sundays was worth it, to have a respite from the uproar he created.

Talking to others who have watched similar outbursts and tantrums in their bosses, I am certain that some young men trigger these incomprehensible rages in older men, as some children—just by being there or looking like a hated relative—attract the same type of venom from natural fathers. In cases like these, at home and in the office, probably the only way out for the young man is to leave.

The role of the son is the most potentially dangerous, the one with the highest stakes, the greatest risks, and yet the most opportunities. If the son's professional needs are greater than his personal needs for a father, he may succeed spectacularly.

He may be lucky enough to become a favorite son. If so, his success may come quickly and easily. If his corporate father leaves, he is unlikely to become special enough to the new executive in charge and he may be forced to leave and find a new position. Wherever he is, in time, he may outgrow the original father, or a new one, and abandon him for a better one.

To rise in the corporate ranks, he may become a father himself, while he is still a favorite son. He may settle old scores with his former sisters and brothers and start new vendettas with potential rivals. He may bully some, he may create his own favorite sons, and he may lock out some others completely.

He may find a new father when he is promoted over the original one. He may humiliate the old man or he may care for him as a real son looks after an aging parent.

As long as he is a son, he will fulfill the new father's fantasy, become an extension of his personality, that secret self that the father wanted to be. His is the second leading role in the corporation, and if he falters, many understudies are waiting in the wings to take over center stage. One of them might just be the daughter.

FOUR

The Daughter:
Growing Up but Not Away

"Girls never fully give up the father or mother relationship, and they are encouraged to continue to identify with their mothers."
—DR. SUSAN LOCKE, *psychologist*

In those five years I spent creating my first office family at the Memphis newspaper, being daughter, sister, and niece to those around me, I was drawn closest to the older men, the fatherly types. They responded to me kindly and authoritatively, assuming full control over my work.

I was not alone, then or now. Because so few women occupy positions of influence in the corporate world, most young women begin their working lives as the symbolic daughters of a male boss—trainable, malleable, controllable daughters. They want to please, to make good, to be good. Unlike their "brothers," they usually take fewer risks. As I was, they are afraid to confront their boss and challenge him —and rightly so, because they are often punished when they try.

Meantime, a young man will be praised for his defiance. Editors used to call that "speaking up, standing up, and telling it, warts and all."

The issues here are power and control. The power and control that many women relinquish so willingly, as I did. The power and control of the male boss of any age over a female employee of any age conditioned to expect and accept his power and control. In his own mind and in the minds of most women in his office, the male boss arrives on the scene with a father's authority and mandate for that power and control.

In turn, without being fully conscious of his attitudes, a male boss views women as kind of universal "daughters" where he sees men as individuals and potential rivals. As a consequence, he acts paternalistic to most of the women in the office and paternal to a few men he wants "to bring along."

Despite all the current talk of mentors, not many women have the support of a male executive personally involved in their careers. Unless they work in unusual offices, they have no female executives to guide and push them, either, as yet—although I hope this will not be true forever.

Why do so many women, seemingly so willingly, relinquish power and control to a male boss? Why are they drawn to an older man and why do they need to be backed with his constant approval?

The need begins in childhood, according to Dr. Susan Locke, a Manhattan psychologist and Baruch College professor who counsels many professional women in her private practice.

Typically, a traditional homemaker mother offers her daughter unconditional love while the breadwinner father offers conditional love, Dr. Locke explained to me. Part of a daughter's self-esteem depends on winning that conditional love from the father, expressed by his approval and praise.

The pattern is often repeated at work, where the daughter frequently needs verification for every professional effort, said Dr. Locke. "She must check on the emotional conditional positive regard of the father, asking, 'Am I doing this right?' 'How should I handle this?' And a conditional regard makes you more uncertain, waiting with bated breath to know whether you did it right or not."

From the start a girl's psychosexual development is more complicated than a boy's. "For the girls, like the boys, the mother is the first love object," Dr. Locke continued. "But a girl is never fully discouraged to give up the identification with the mother, as the boy is, to become more like his father. A girl's relationship with her mother is also more ambivalent. By the time she is involved with her father and the mother is an outsider, how can she fully hate her mother, the person who was her first love, her first caretaker?

"Girls never fully give up the father or mother relationship, and they are encouraged to continue to identify with their mothers."

A woman's career is shaped by the first thirty years of confusion and misunderstanding in the father-daughter relationship, believes Dr. William S. Appleton, psychiatrist and assistant clinical professor of psychiatry at Harvard Medical School. Analyzing a father's influence over a daughter's life span in *Fathers and Daughters* (Doubleday, 1981), Dr. Appleton says, "The little girl saw one father, the adolescent a second, the adult a third. . . . I have learned that it takes a woman until the age of thirty to completely understand her relationship to her father."

At the beginning of her career, a young woman works for a male boss usually about the same age as her father. If she understands her early relationship with her father, she will be able to understand her relationship to her bosses and correct any problems. "It is not that the older man behind the desk reminds her of her father because he looks like him, but that her expectations and attitudes are automatically colored by the inequality in the power between them," says Dr. Appleton.

He compares a woman's career stages to those of her life: starting out as a new employee (childhood), progressing to a semi-independent position (adolescence), and, finally, becoming a manager (adult).

A woman may project onto her boss the little-girl expectations she had of her real father. If she was adored and praised, she may expect that at work; if she was criticized or ignored, she may avoid her boss or overreact to his criticism.

"The adult woman executive has completed her second cycle of maturation," Dr. Appleton concludes. "The first was in relation to her father as she advanced from his adored little girl to an adolescent shifting back and forth between dependence and independence, to an adult who is separate but equal. Similarly, in her career, she began as a child full of promise, needing direction and training, grew to an adolescent capable of some responsibility but requiring limits and guidance, and finally became a mature person capable of leadership."

He paints a rosy picture. Valuable, but rosy nevertheless. Because it assumes that the norm in corporate life is a male boss who wants a mature woman, separate but equal, and capable of leadership—a boss who does not want to keep her an adolescent or punish her for growing older. On the other side of the coin, he also assumes that every woman eventually wants to relinquish a daughter's dependency or knows how to tip the balance of power between herself and her boss.

Human beings often make decisions based on their feelings, then justify those feelings with "facts," Dr. Squires had emphasized. As I have learned, office life is often dominated by heady psychological needs of bosses and employees. Because a man's need to control is often met by a young woman's need to *be* controlled, women can find it difficult to grow up mentally, to grow out of the helpless, sweet, dependent Good Girl to become the adolescent, then the "mature person."

Among friends and strangers in corporate offices, I found women playing the role of office daughter at all ages. While some of them enjoyed the privileged inequality of the little girl, many others played her with resentment, in deep conflict with their true selves, yet not knowing what else to do. They were confused about the limits of daughterhood, about when and how to end it.

In examining the role of the daughter in the office, I found that although most women are only daughters in the generic sense, a few of them had true office "fathers" who intervened in their lives and changed their careers. Some of them had "stumbled" onto a father figure and some had made a deliberate search for a father, like the young men. As they explained how they played out the role of the daughter, all attributed much of their professional growth to that relationship. They knew that it provided great insights into corporate life, but they were ambivalent about its benefits.

Elizabeth, at twenty-six, is nearly six feet tall. Her wavy brown hair is shoulder-length, and her slim hips are usually encased in a tight leather skirt. Last year she became an assistant editor of one of the nation's most prestigious magazines. She was hired three years ago by a senior editor who taught at her graduate school.

"I was Tony's student in a college writing course," she told me hesitantly, unsure of where our conversation was going. "Right from the first, he took a liking to me, and I to him. Maybe it was because my mother had taught me not to kowtow, but to talk back, just enough to provoke a man's interest, and in a nice way.

"After I graduated, he got me a job here at his magazine. He told everyone—the whole staff—that I was his 'star pupil.'

"Now I have proved myself. They put me in charge of the articles department. But he's still running around, bragging, telling people, 'I made her what she is today.' I don't even see him that much now, but I know that he still feels like my father. Sometimes he'll pass me in the hall and ask me, 'What would you do without me?' I hate that."

Although she is a reluctant "daughter" to Tony, Elizabeth values his interest in her and would never discourage it. "I couldn't be here today without him," she readily admits.

She is much more grateful to another male editor who left the magazine six months ago. He gave her confidence in herself as well as practical help. "I was even more of a daughter figure to Marshall. After I had been here a couple of weeks, he started hanging around my desk, teasing me with stuff like 'What oddball life-style story are you working on today?' He liked molding young women, especially. He used to clean up my copy and get rid of all the boring adverbs and long-winded phrases. But he would treat me like a professional, and I could disagree with him.

"He wanted me to be in his stable here, and if he had stayed, he would have gotten me transferred to the magazine's entertainment section. He was a queen-maker type, and he gave me a lot of confidence in myself. He would say offhand things like 'You know, you're perfectly capable of writing screenplays.' "

Elizabeth finds the daughter pose confining, and at times, degrading. "But what can you do?" she asked. "I guess you fall into a role once and it's expected of you forever."

Too many women believe that. It cripples them emotionally and professionally.

Will it cripple Marge? I doubt that she will ever escape the juvenile role she has been stuck in for eleven years. After her divorce and remarriage, with both children in high school, Marge started work in an office-supply firm, and progressed rapidly from trainee to clerk to secretary to saleswoman to vice-president for sales. Today, she develops programs for the company's entire sales force and travels across the country giving demonstration seminars about the products.

Relatively new to the business world, she is grateful for the opportunities her bosses have "given" her and she looks to these men to point out guidelines. Marge justifies this as standard corporate tactics. "I see that most of the men on my level—which is fairly high—have someone to reach to, and so do I. I have called Peter for his opinion and advice even when he's at home, sick. But I have learned that if you ask him a question, you had better be ready to do what he tells you. If you know the right questions to ask him, he can be very generous with his time. Once I heard him say, 'I'll never help that guy anymore because he never pays any attention to me.'

"You always have to go to him, and make it your business to give him an opportunity to shine on you. It's always his move, but you have to open the door. You can't go in naked and barefoot, as it were. He is very quiet, and narrow-minded, discriminatory, opinionated, formal, and unforgiving. He is only an assistant vice-president but he has become a kind of father to several vice-presidents. He has even groomed our next president."

Marge, who is now thirty-nine, thinks that she has been given excellent support, as she put it, "for a woman my age." She found her "father" by accident.

"The senior officer who hired me said to Peter, 'I want you to look after her.' Well, Peter happened to like me and said, 'I'm going to tell you that this is the way things appear to be, but this is not the way things are.' Then he began to point out different ways of behaving.

Once at a dinner meeting, he whispered to me, 'Look around. The people in power do the listening, not the talking.'

"Once I got up in a meeting to present my ideas on sales strategy, and he flagged me down, motioning me to shut up. So I wound down my speech and sat down. I was furious. How dare he cut me off? That afternoon he called me into his office and told me why. 'You never give your ideas away in a meeting. Send a memo and send copies of it to the people you want to know about it.' "

Marge now has found a second man to help her. "I guess I gave another man in the office my permission to be a 'father' to me when I asked his advice—although he's much younger than Peter, who is in his late fifties. This man is in his early thirties. After my first presentation, Fred said to me, 'You were terrific. But be careful. When you're good, everybody tries to tear you apart.' From the beginning, I got approval and advice from him. Now, I think that he is becoming more of a brother than a father to me, as I get on a higher level."

Not many women have had office "mothers" with authority comparable to the "fathers" they worked for. That is why I especially wanted to see Edith, a go-getter who has held various jobs in broadcasting as secretary, promotion writer, advertising copywriter, marketing manager—several with women bosses—over the last twenty-two years.

Edith, who is forty-three, talked about the men, even the worst ones, with more affection than the women.

"On my first job, I guess I had a permissive older 'father,' about sixty, who did not interfere with me at all, who had a 1960s approach to parenting. The upshot was that the rivalry among the younger people in his office went unchecked. There was no real discipline and there were no controls.

"Then we got a new boss who was just forty, closer to the age of most of the people in the office. His orientation was to a boys' club, a peer group, and I was completely left out.

"Later on, I had a tough boss, a real disciplinarian, verbally abusive. But the people who could work with him felt that he was inspiring and brilliant. He knew what he wanted and he could articulate it and get people to produce. He held everything together when the radio station's relations with the network back in New York were falling apart.

"Despite his shortcomings, he still commanded respect. I haven't heard from him in years, but I still remember his support and encouragement. Maybe it's the same as with someone who is dead, I only remember the good things. I have often wondered if I reminded him of his daughter. I know that I would pay to work for him again. The people in his department were always right, and they always had his backing. It made you feel indomitable.

"He would say to us, 'Be there when I need you, and get results.' There were no office politics. It was an ideal situation. There were no benefits in that company, yet he kept people for twenty-five years or more. He provided something that you can't advertise and can't buy. He encouraged creative people. There was an electric atmosphere in the office and we felt that we were an elite group.

"But when he moved his office to the West Coast and I could not go there, I found that working with him had set me up for subsequent unhappy relationships. I wanted the world to be like that. It would be so nice to feel that support again. But you can't go back to that situation.

"In my next job, I had a mean, abrasive boss. Nobody could be near him for very long, much less get close to him. He treated everybody badly. So all of us left that company after two or three years at most. Including me.

"In my present job, I feel like an outcast. My original boss, whom I respected, was promoted to manager of a bigger station and my option is to make nice to his rival, who took over, a man I despise because he's such a jerk. Besides, he distrusts women. Yet I have to work with him and I'm trying to change my feelings about him."

In all these jobs, Edith unconditionally accepted her boss's opinion of her work and his attitudes toward her as a person. She attributed this dependence to her failure to come to terms with her feelings about her own father.

"I didn't have an approving father," she told me. "Maybe it was because I was a tomboy and wanted to be just like him. I wanted to fix things around the house the way he did, and to write poetry and to sail the boat the way he did. I demanded that he teach me how to drive the jeep he bought when I was fourteen. But of course he couldn't and wouldn't. I didn't realize that I was too young and my legs were too short and he didn't explain why he couldn't. But I remember wanting to consume him, I loved him so."

I was disappointed that Edith had so little to say about the women executives she worked for. "They just cloned the problems of men," Edith told me bitterly. "I was in an all-woman office once. Everybody asked advice from one woman who treated us all like little children. Maybe the mother-child relationship is more infantile. You never get to be the peer of a mother.

"In another place, a woman boss my age who had no children was forever urging me to comb my hair and wear more expensive clothes. She started tremendous rivalry among us. Most of all, she was just too much a presence in our everyday lives."

Edith has been married twice but has no children. Perhaps that is why she feels that you cannot be a peer of an office "mother" if you are a woman. I think that it's easier if you are a mother yourself, because being a mother gives you authority and dignity, or perhaps more of an adult aura.

Even if you are not a mother at home, it is still possible to be an office colleague to an older woman who wants to mother. It can be difficult, though. Like Edith, many women (and men, too) resent older women bosses whom they see as meddling "mothers."

But attitudes like this will not survive much longer, as more young people entering the corporate world find female bosses right from the start, and as more children have mothers who are also corporate executives.

Years pass, and it becomes increasingly difficult to maintain the daughter role, as Anne is discovering. An interior designer who has worked in several of New York's finest department stores for thirty-five years, Anne at fifty-five is still soft and blond but plumper than she was a few years ago. Today she is looking back over her life as we sit on white wicker patio chairs overlooking the lawn in a fashionable Long Island suburb. We are sipping Bloody Marys and nibbling pretzels.

"I have always had an office father, wherever I worked, because I guess I needed one," Anne declared bluntly. "Or felt as if I couldn't get along without one. And I have always had submerged 'Electra' feelings toward these men.

"For women of my generation, manipulation of men started with the first job. I was twenty. Bill, my first boss, was only twenty-eight, but I treated him like a father. It was part of the act. He treated me like a favorite daughter. He had hired me, so I was the apple of his eye. He was so pleased whenever I succeeded. It was all part of the routine.

"I would never speak up at a meeting, the way I would normally talk when only women were around. I think that's why we women have developed this technique of speaking so differently to our own sex. And I think that when we finally do talk to a man the way we talk to a woman, that's when we fall in love.

"I married and became pregnant, and when I got there late in the morning because I was so tired in my fourth month, Bill told me I could just come in whenever I wanted to, and not to worry. Thirty-five years later, I still remember the way he looked, when he was so sweet to me. To this day, I think about him. There's still that relationship that exists."

Anne stopped to pour another Bloody Mary and began to think about her real father. She glowed.

"I had a very strong father relationship. My father was probably the most important man in my life and I could not have had my first affair if he had not died. He and my older brother disagreed a lot. I think my brother and my mother had the classic relationship and so did my father and I. I always felt that he loved me and approved of me.

"My father never yelled at me, never slapped me. Well, only once, in my entire life. My brother and I shared a room and one night we were giggling. Our parents told us to be quiet. We didn't—or couldn't —and my father came in and gave both of us a spanking. Really, it was only a slap on the tush. He was always my closest friend, my best critic, my guide, my mentor, my everything. One of the things I regret most about my daughter and my divorce is that she couldn't have the same kind of relationship with her father."

I visualized the beautiful and troubled friend beside me as a little girl adoring her father. Imagine! Being lucky enough to have a father, and then getting one who adored you. I envied her. I asked, "When you went to work, were you unconsciously trying to recreate the relationship with your father?"

Apparently, the idea had occurred to her many times. "My father was still alive, but I'm sure that every man in an executive position was a spin-off of my father."

It seemed to me that Anne was locked in an adolescent state of development with her own father. I went back to Dr. Locke to ask if Anne and women like her with strong feelings for their fathers were doomed to transfer those feelings to every man they worked for.

"Not necessarily," was Dr. Locke's response. Although many of us remain immature in our relationships with our real fathers, we do not have to play the good little girl or the adolescent rebel with our male bosses.

Dr. Locke viewed the clinging to the role of the daughter as part of the "fear of success" syndrome. "Women have this fear that as they become more effective, more competent professionally, they have given up their right to lean on someone. The more successful they are, the more frightened they are of giving up that female privilege which men don't have—to fail, to lean on someone. You can't imagine the men in an organization saying, 'If I can't do this, would you do it for me?' Or 'Would you help me?' Or 'Take a look at my work.'

"That uncertainty," she said, "is a luxury that women have that both gets them off the hook if they make a mistake and is a form of reinforcement of a relationship with a male mentor who appreciates the opportunity to show that he is a good father. On the other hand, men in the organization have to make it on their own, to prove that they are executive stuff, to prove their independence."

Anne decided to return to work when her daughter was a year old. "I got a job at a small store in New Jersey and I think I may still have a silent crush on the guy who hired me. He was not even ten years older than I was. Every morning we would have a training session, matching wits over colors and fabrics for our clients, and I would look forward to it.

"He fired me after I told him I wanted Christmas week off to go with my husband and daughter to Bermuda. He said I had deceived him into believing I was staying in town for the holidays. But I don't resent him for that, although I was furious at the time. I always ask about him when I come across people who know him. I think I've always had a real thing about this man. He's brilliant, and powerful, and eccentric, and nuts. He, more than anyone, was a father.

"In my next job, there was a whole structure of men. The first one was the head of personnel who hired me, who became a powerful vice-president. He was a very fatherly man. Now what do I mean by 'fatherly'? Proud, sponsoring, giving advice. On my part, it meant not really sticking my neck out, and trying to please, then consciously or subconsciously being delighted when I got the pat on the head.

"I was one of the few women at that store. I think I happened to fall into a daughter role. I was very pretty, still very soft in my behavior and attitudes, and not particularly aggressive. I replaced a woman they didn't like, and if they didn't like you, they put you in Siberia, in jobs where they didn't have to talk to you.

"You had to be pretty to be a daughter. And you had to be bright, but not show it. Not challenge them obviously with your intelligence. Complement them, complement with an 'e' and make them look good. Then you got the pat on the head, literally, sometimes.

"The man I worked for, the store's assistant vice-president, I had a real crush on, but I never did anything about it. I was not promiscuous. I had what I called 'silent affairs' with my bosses—not sexual relationships, but emotional ones.

"My boss, Mark, was one of those screaming maniac creative people who could eat you alive, but I never really got any of that, even when he came back from a meeting where his ideas were stomped on. He was always very gentle with me, as if I were fragile.

"I did not see the store president more than five times during those years, but his reputation as a tyrant was well-deserved. He knew all about me, and I was scared of him. One day in a meeting with him and fifteen men, we presented our ideas for promoting the store's interior design services, and he didn't say a word for two hours. That meant that our presentation was superb. If he didn't rip it apart and us along with it, that meant he liked it, and that was a rare event.

"Anyway, as I was leaving, he put his arm around me, fully aware of his reputation as a man- and woman-eating tiger, and he laughed, 'Now that wasn't too bad, was it?' I smiled up at him, and answered, 'No,' and cuddled up like a little girl. I was delighted to be noticed by him, and I blushed, the whole bit. That was my reward. I got the hugs; the men got the raises.

"With the exception of that president, all the men who were my 'fathers' were my age, or within a few years. Which is crazy. I have to take responsibility for creating these relationships. There's no question about it. This is the way I can manipulate the men. Subconsciously, I just went into these relationships. And that way, I got what I wanted, I guess. I advanced in my job. They worried about me. They renewed my contract. They gave me a little more money.

"They even took care of me. I remember once when I was going through my separation from my husband and I was at a meeting where everyone was nasty and critical. One man was just a little too nasty to me and I started crying uncontrollably—something I had never done before. He sent everyone out of the room, and sat down and talked to me. And for a few minutes, he was mine, all mine."

I asked Anne what she assumed the men got out of being a father to her.

Not much, she thought. Fatherhood was just a familiar, comfortable relationship. "I think it's a role that our generation of men was taught. Big brother taking over the father role. I think that when women came into the business world, this was the only way that men knew how to treat women. They saw how their fathers treated their sisters. How else were they going to do it?

"Except for the old bitch, and they certainly didn't want to be like her, women had very few role models. They felt they had to behave the way they behaved with their fathers and brothers. This whole transition period we're in now, with women doing their own networking, speaking up for themselves, taking different roles, is so intimidating to men—no, wait a minute . . . men aren't that scared that women are going to take their jobs, but they just don't know how to handle this totally new kind of relationship and they are so uncomfortable with it. Because it doesn't come out of a familial relationship, there's no prototype for it. They think we're offensive and loud and they don't know how to handle it."

By the time Anne reached forty-five she was divorced and living alone in her sleek, customed-designed glass and cedar suburban ranch house. Her daughter was off at college and Anne switched firms again, this time working for one specializing in office interiors.

"There I didn't have a father-daughter relationship and maybe that's why things didn't work out at first. I guess Matt didn't appeal to me as a 'father.' Maybe it was because I was living alone and becoming more independent. We didn't like each other. He was not supportive and, in fact, I thought he acted like a traitor. He resented it when I gave directions to the construction crews. He would drive by the next day and make them do it his way."

Eventually, Matt left to start his own business and in walked Ross, characterized by Anne as "anything but what a father should be, completely irresponsible, a gambler, a womanizer."

Suddenly, she had outgrown her father. "I became a teenager, questioning his wisdom. I no longer saw him as perfect. Suddenly I had to be careful, be wary. And I no longer trusted him as the expert in everything." Anne was growing up, and scared to admit it. Scared to face the consequences of becoming an adult woman in the business world.

I wanted to hear Anne's opinion about the differences between office sons and daughters. It seemed to me that office fathers and sons have a special, personal relationship while office fathers and daughters, with some exceptions, have a more generalized and diffused relationship.

A woman relates as a daughter to several male authority figures without feeling like *the* daughter to any specific father. Yet a man working alongside her considers most male authorities his peers or semiequals, but feels like *the* son to one special executive.

Likewise, male executives of any age may view nearly all women as daughters to be taught and trained, but will tend to see the men around them as distinct individuals, either colleagues or rivals, then pick one or two to be *the* "son."

Anne had noted these differences, too. "The sons are part of that male network of closed doors, special lunches, camaraderie, and so forth. The women are just there, but not as close. It is like father and son going off to the ball game, and then father and daughter having their own special thing. But women at work are just not part of the club. They're spared certain harsh facts of life, like not having to understand about cash flow, but they don't get close to power. They're doing the first draft of the work, which is perfectly fine, but Daddy has to put his mark on it and change it.''

The age question eventually dominates a woman's working life, said Anne, who has resigned herself to this after denying it for so many years.

"Sons can get older, but daughters dare not," she told me. "The younger a woman, the more a daughter she is to a man. Age twenty is ideal; at thirty you've got to be careful; at age forty it's okay if you hide it. The father chooses the daughter, but the son eyes the father and waits for his choice to be confirmed.

"From the sons, the father wants loyalty, imitation, and learning. From the daughters, he wants titillation, adoration, and if not sex play, at least flirtation. What they really get out of it is a small kingdom, and a certain sexual adoration. They want to see it in her eyes."

Anne is in the interior design business for herself now, but business is slow. I was surprised when she attributed some of her financial troubles to the loss of a father, but she told me that she functions best as a daughter and would find it degrading to be looked on as a "mother."

"If I had a father-daughter relationship with my clients, who are mostly businessmen," she said, "I would get more business. It has worked for me in the past. I need the pattern. But if I had a really strong father relationship again, it would be an affair relationship, I think."

How long can a woman keep on being the daughter?

"I don't know. Maybe, in one sense, it really doesn't have much to do with age, as long as there is a man willing to play the role. I can remember when I was in an office with a woman who was seventy years old. I watched her go into the meetings with our thirty-five-year-old hot-shot president, all dolled up, powdering her nose, making sure she looked okay. And it worked, to some degree. The men like it, no matter what age they are. I've seen thirty-year-old guys coming on as fathers to women of fifty. It gives them authority. And it gives the women protection."

Finally, I wanted to know if Anne chose her fathers or if they chose her because she was young and blond and beautiful and smart—just the kind of daughter any man would want.

"I suspect I chose them, and directed the relationship. I suspect that I was the manipulator. And they fell into that role, happy to be manipulated. As a little girl I must have manipulated my father like that, away from my brother. To the day my father died, and even now, I think my brother is jealous of that personal, close relationship my father and I had.

"All this affected the men I fell in love with, too. I don't think I could ever have a lover who was not a father figure. I'm never attracted to a man unless he has some sort of power, or money, or has more courage, or more knowledge, or something more than I do. He must be my guide, my teacher, my protector. And this is in spite of the fact that I am a very domineering personality.

"I usually avoid relationships with other men in the office. They don't matter and never have. I head for the top. I get along with the others superficially. When a man wants to be my 'father,' he is soft and kind and wants to do that patting on the head and I sense that he wants to be my protector. But if he's not at the level I want my father to be, I'm just coolly polite to him. It's worked very well."

Maybe, I protested, you're giving these men too much credit for your success and denigrating your own talent that got you this far.

"No question about it, I produced good designs, the kind of work they wanted," Anne replied. "But it's always been under their sponsorship. When I wanted to go into business for myself, I realized that I was not succeeding because I was alone. In this business the men just do not take you seriously. How many women do you know who have their own firms? Very few. It can be the same contract, basically, but they just don't take you seriously enough without the sponsorship of a man. It's almost like the father presenting his daughter to society. She can't come out by herself."

The dependent daughter fantasy that persists into a woman's forties and fifties keeps her perpetually infanticized. For if she continues to perceive herself as a child, and is always perceived that way by her bosses, then she will always be that little girl, never taken as seriously as her male colleagues. She will be cuddled, patted on the head, then discarded (gently, of course) when she no longer serves Daddy's purpose.

Equally as damaging, she may, like Anne, believe that she must get younger and blonder and thinner while the men around her get older and grayer and heavier. Aging is disgraceful and not to be tolerated in a daughter. As Barbara Walters once commented, she is considered the "grande dame" of television while Dan Rather, who is older, is looked on as the "new boy on the block." Imagine Barbara Walters still being allowed to face the TV cameras when she is close to sixty-five, as Walter Cronkite was when he retired—although he seemed much older.

Part of the problem is image, and what a woman is supposed to be at a particular age. We all have our own ideas, but it is the ideas of male bosses that count at the present.

As long as her need for approval is stronger than the need for self-expression, a woman will always be trapped in that subordinate daughter role, said Dr. Locke.

Somewhere in her mid-thirties, Dr. Locke feels, a woman is usually "ready to fly" out of the daughter role. The father figure who was once so helpful now seems to be holding her back.

But breaking away without tears and slamming of doors is hard to do. For both of them.

It takes a wise and generous "father" to understand the need for separation and not to be threatened by it. It takes a wise and generous "daughter" to understand an older man's fears about the decline of his own career, with all that means in limited power and prestige.

But, says Dr. Locke, if a woman keeps on thinking of her boss as a powerful daddy figure, instead of as a human being with his own anxieties, she will find it nearly impossible to leave him.

She must also be willing to pay the price of flying solo. "Otherwise, she is like the woman who says she would like a job and more independence but her husband won't let her have it. What she is saying is that she is unwilling to deal with the confrontation. Like a teenager, she is not willing to take the responsibility for the consequences of her actions. She wants to rebel but she wants to be protected from the consequences.

"Sometimes," concludes Dr. Locke, "a woman who is a daughter has to accept the falling-out of a relationship, accept other people's anger, and give up the right to be dependent and thus prove that she is an adult."

It may seem easier, more natural, and safer for a woman to remain a daughter at work. Yet for the sake of her success in her career and her personal maturity, a woman must break that bond, stop projecting her feelings about fathers and mothers onto her bosses, and—even harder —stop the projections of their feelings onto her.

In her own natural family, she may cling to the father or mother relationship and identify with her mother (usually the more dependent of the two parents). But the clinging, the identification, and the dependency do not have to accompany her into the office and color her relationships with older men and women. She can recognize the dangers of allowing that to happen and make a deliberate effort to break that destructive pattern.

Once a woman reaches her mid-thirties, the daughter role is usually no longer appropriate and can keep her in a dependent, submissive position, waiting for the pats on the head and the smiles of approval. The mid-thirties are the time for her to move on, assume another role if that is possible, or else leave for a new company to create a new character role for herself.

The daughter. It may be the right role and, possibly, even inevitable, for some women beginning their careers. But it is not the right role for a lifetime of working. If played too long, it can typecast a woman permanently in a supporting role, stunting her personality and her career. In the corporate family, as in the real one, a daughter must grow up and grow away from the parents in order to find her own place in life. Perhaps she makes the break by becoming a mother.

FIVE

The Mother:
Needing to Be Needed

"I see so many women who have it all—looks, brains, and talent—and yet they wind up playing the most subservient roles, getting coffee and cleaning up. Maybe they have a distorted identification with their own mothers. Maybe they have a fear of their own autonomy and fear of healthy assertion. Maybe they have a conflict managing their own competence."
—DR. HARVEY BAROCAS, *psychologist*

Mother is our first love object in life, and therefore, whether we are male or female, we tend to marry the person most like our mother. So one theory goes. Or, according to another theory, we are attracted to the one who most resembles our "opposite sex" parent.

Take the theories or leave them, but you cannot ignore your feelings about mothers. Especially office mothers.

I was still in my teens when my mother died, and she has always been a shadowy figure. I am never quite sure whether my memories of her reflect my own dimmest childhood feelings or whether she really was the way I think she was. As I grew older, I visualized the perfect mother in my imagination. I knew exactly what she should look like and how she should behave. I spent hours inventing her—aided in my fantasies by radio soap operas and magazine portraits of "typical" American families. In high school I would silently "adopt" friends' mothers, often enjoying their company and their conversations far more than their daughters'.

Curiously, I never wanted a mother at work as I wanted a father and, to a lesser extent, brothers and sisters. I never wanted to *be* a mother at work, either, and I resented it when I, at about age thirty and a mother of young children myself, first began to be treated as one.

After a while it seemed a natural progression to go from being a daughter and, more and more often, a sister to being a kind of mother-friend, and it was comfortable in many ways. Office mates of both sexes and all ages came to me to talk over union rules or journalism ethics or personal problems. I liked the prestige, the authority, the power, but, most of all, the attention I got from giving my advice and opinions. I needed to be needed.

Of all the family parts played out in offices, the mother role is the least dependent on age or status. Men and women of forty-three or fifty-three easily turn to a sympathetic, understanding woman of thirty-three, even a newcomer, and request some "motherly" help, which she will usually be delighted to give.

I certainly was delighted for several years. Until I realized that this relationship can harm "mother" and "child."

When I joined a small weekly, I inherited a beguiling and flirtatious young woman assistant who introduced herself sweetly, tossed her glossy black curls, and warned me with a devilish grin that she could work only "under close supervision." She was right. I tried to arrive at the office early in order to organize her duties from highest to lowest priority. Even if I wrote everything down on a yellow legal pad, Judy still took off at ten each morning, wandering around the office, charming the salesmen and the printers with her silly jokes and sensational figure.

Meantime, our stringers were calling in with stories to be typed and our readers were lining up with engagement pictures. I boiled inside as I struggled to handle the phone calls and the visitors. When Judy returned to her desk, she would involve me for twenty minutes in a discussion of her love life and the battles with her parents over her boyfriends.

I was not old enough to be Judy's mother (we were only ten years apart in age) but that was the role she had selected for me and was convinced she needed me to play. She wanted to be advised, babied, told what to do and how to do it every day. Instead of being delighted to help out, as I had been in other jobs, with other people, I was becoming deeply resentful. I was irritated at having to do her job—plus mine—angry at myself for allowing her to play the spoiled child, and terrified of scolding her or firing her. Even worse, I was beginning to look like the office patsy, the weak and helpless mommy who allows youngsters to walk all over her. Others in the office were coming to me for advice, but ignoring me when I wanted them to change the angle on the Monday night town-board-meeting story.

Every day it became clearer that this relationship foisted on me by one employee was seriously damaging my credibility, her efficiency, and the entire office operation. But how was I going to get out of it?

By playing my real role—Judy's boss. In this case a boss who becomes a detached mother, a mother who lets the child fly by herself, even if she has to push that child out of the nest. I made a list of Judy's daily and weekly jobs, from answering the phones to typing the letters. When she lost it in three days I just shrugged and suggested that she write down her own list. And I walked away when she started describing last night's date at the drive-in.

At last I found the courage to write her a note saying that unless the situation improved, we would no longer need her. (I still could not bear personal confrontations.) In the note I pointed out that the paper could not afford to pay her for wandering the halls.

My strategy worked. Judy stayed at her desk, stopped asking me for help, and no longer involved me in her personal life. I regained my lost authority. I gained an employee. But I lost a daughter. Until she left a year later, Judy remained distant and sullen. It was not a bad trade-off, although a few times I looked back longingly on the days when Judy laughed and joked with us, and depended on me.

The mother role is not only less contingent on age or status than the other roles are, but it is also the one most diffused and idiosyncratic. Isn't that just the paradoxical, quixotic nature of mothers? And children, too. Brothers and sisters will react differently to the same mother. Throughout our lifetimes our relationship with our mothers is more ambivalent.

Although individual personalities and styles can be completely different and changeable, I found that office mothers come in three basic models: the nurturing wife-mommy, the tough executive father-mother, and the Big Mama owner-mother.

We have all encountered the traditional "wife-mommy," played with great flair by executive secretaries and executive assistants who often guard their "masters" like dogs protecting the office gates.

Lois is a good example. She is the executive assistant to a longtime politician who runs a state building agency. Lois knows all there is to know about union contracts and the price of bricks and concrete. In her boss's name she negotiates everything from overtime to extended delivery time and the contractors always send her boxes of chocolates and bottles of perfume at Christmas. She writes her boss's birthday cards to his children at college, buys his wife's anniversary earrings, and accepts or rejects his invitations to speak at political events.

"Not only that," she eagerly added over a tuna-fish sandwich at her desk, "I also listen to him complain about the contractors, I congratulate him when we finish another industrial park, and I go out to lunch with him to celebrate when we win out over the union guys. He needs me and he depends on me and that makes me feel good. I like being in the center of things and I don't understand these women who think it's so terrible to bring your boss his coffee when you get to make the major business decisions for him and he trusts you. I like working for a man who says he couldn't get along without me."

But Lois—hear the other side! Not all men want a wife-mommy, and, in fact, some deeply resent all that personal attention. Executives like Gary, who owns a furniture company, bitterly complained to me about "smothering mothering." Gary fairly spit out his words the day he described his secretary. "She wants to open my mail even when it's marked 'personal,' and she wants a full report on the restaurants I eat in when I go out of town and what hotels I stayed in, and whether they put through her messages promptly. I had to install a private line in my office to keep her from listening in on my phone conversations. God, I wish I knew how to get rid of her."

Too many women (not all of them secretaries) get into this role too deeply, according to New York career counselor Sharon Bermon, who often jokes that she feels like a marriage counselor and not a career counselor.

"Women complain to me that their bosses never notice them, or never talk to them," Ms. Bermon said to me. "Sometimes they even talk about 'withholding their love,' just like wives do.

"I see a lot of women who follow men around, travel with them, do everything for them, clean up their mess, and have a sort of mother-slave relationship with them. Women like this think of men as children who must be taken care of.

"One woman, an executive secretary who also had the title of sales manager, couldn't figure out her place in the office. When she came to see me, she talked like a wife, saying that she never got her boss's exclusive attention," recalled Ms. Bermon. "She quit once, but he persuaded her to return. Then she felt guilty."

Ms. Bermon and other counselors advise women in this kind of dilemma to stop and take stock of themselves, to become more goal-oriented at work, and examine their feelings about dependence or independence on the job.

Confronted with the two choices, some women will finally come to the conclusion that, painful as it is to give up dependency, they must try to achieve success on their own.

Many others will decide that they want to continue the more traditional and dependent wife-mommy role at work.

After all, most women come from traditional families where the father's needs come first. These women often prefer the supporting roles of nurse, secretary, paralegal, or dental hygenist, the indirect achievers alongside men who are direct achievers.

"Some women who don't have children put all their energy into nurturing in the office," said Ms. Bermon. "Sometimes they become jealous and possessive, getting their identity from a man. It's a territorial thing, like allowing no one into your kitchen. They are the first ones there in the morning and the last to leave at night. They make everybody angry but you can't fire them because they are the only ones who know where the paper clips are.''

Why is it that with all the breakthroughs women at work have made in the past decade, so many still find their job satisfaction and personal fulfillment tending male needs? I was puzzled, and so was psychologist Harvey Barocas, who shared these observations with me: ''I see so many women who have it all—looks, brains, and talent—and yet they wind up playing the most subservient roles, getting coffee and cleaning up. Maybe they have a distorted identification with their own mothers. Maybe they have a fear of their own autonomy and fear of healthy assertion. Maybe they have a conflict managing their competence.''

I think that these explanations only partly solve the puzzle. Women, as they have been from the beginning in the workplace, are also responding to society's powerful expectations of service from a woman, and that need to be needed that is instilled in us so early.

Another type of woman is appearing more and more in the corporate family today—one I call the ''tough executive father-mother'' or the ''modern breakthrough mother'' who slips in and out of the role at her own pleasure.

As far away as she can be in attitude and style from the ''wife-mommy,'' this woman, usually in her forties or fifties, working as a middle-level or senior executive, is making a serious, deliberate effort to create the best of motherhood, especially for younger women whom she sees as younger versions of herself. She hopes to spare them the pain and frustration she herself endured en route to the top.

This new breed is well aware of the traps implicit in the traditional ''wife-mommy'' role and in the ''nurturing mother'' part I was forced into, and she is determined to avoid them. She does not play the tough parent constantly, but only when she senses that it is necessary to get across a point or to give advice (unsolicited, perhaps, but critical) to a younger colleague. She takes risks in personal relationships as well as in business.

Often, she is thrust unwillingly into the role by young, desperate colleagues, or by situations where the role is essential, in her opinion. She sees it as a limited, fleeting opportunity to teach a uniquely valuable lesson or to encourage younger women (and on rare occasions, men) on their way up. In this she is like the office father who yearns to share his wisdom and experience with the younger generation.

"People come to me and want to talk," said Marianne, vice-president of a medical equipment firm. At forty-two Marianne has ten years of experience in management and in our conversation she stressed that she has learned how to be tough. Very tough.

"I play the part of mother-who-is-a-father to the women in my office who come to see me, because basically I want to pass it on, and see them get ahead. There is so much they need to know, and so little time to find it out.

"But I am a father, not a nurturing earth mother. I think you can make a big difference in someone's life. For instance, one day a woman who felt slighted by her boss's careless, critical remark told me that she was resigning immediately, that she just couldn't take his 'cruelty.' I advised her to calm down, to assume for a day that she was staying and to do all the things she would have done, then decide tomorrow whether or not she wanted to leave. Well, she just needed a little time to lick her wounds. She stayed, of course, and is doing well. In fact, she just got a raise."

Like many of the new executive mothers, Marianne is not threatened by competition from a younger woman or man, and she resists the temptation to allow anyone to lean on her. She easily separates her concerns as a real mother from the concerns of a corporate mother. "I delight in my assistant. She is the same age as my son, who is twenty-four. But I expect more out of her than I do of him. I want everyone who works for me to grow and be promoted. I will say to the young men I hire for the staff, 'If you were my son, I would be delighted if you could take this opportunity.' But I do not think of them as my sons.

"In fact, when people around me start to lean on me and become dependent, I say, 'I am not your mother and I am not nice.' That statement is made by Marine Corps drill sergeants. They also say, and so do I, 'This is not your home.' When I say that, people are surprised, for they think I will be a nice place in the storm. But instead I get angry with them for doing something wrong and I don't protect them from the boss."

A secret and valuable use of the mother role, I discovered, is in defusing office sexuality.

Sex is the number one interpersonal issue in offices today. Several years ago I heard Margaret Mead propose a unique solution during a speech she made before business leaders. Like the family, the modern corporation should develop incest taboos, she told them.

"If we're ever going to have men and women on an equal basis, with men over men and women over men, we have to develop decent sex mores," she declared. "We've got to stop the exploitation that is usual—the young men who prey on older women, the middle-aged men and younger women, the office wife, the Christmas parties. We're going to have to get rid of all this."

Mothers can turn a potentially "incestuous" father-daughter office relationship into a camaraderie between a boss and a caring friend. It is an effective style of coping with sexual harassment, but it must be skillfully handled without subservience or dependence.

Harriet, a senior account executive for an advertising agency billing $27 million annually, spends her days and much of her nights in a living-room size office on the nineteenth floor of a Park Avenue skyscraper in New York. The walls are the palest robin's-egg blue and the furniture is upholstered in leather the color of golden butter with armrests in sleek modern chrome.

Back when she was sixteen Harriet learned how to remove sex from work in her first job as a summer switchboard operator for the biggest insurance agency in town. The biggest insurance agency, naturally, hired the largest number of agents.

"I got some real big shocks on that first job, let me tell you," she said, flashing green-gray eyes, pushing back her dark brown pageboy and sinking down beside me on the leather couch.

"I discovered that every man who wanted to be my 'father' did not really want to be my 'father.' He wanted to climb in bed with me and cover it up by appearing to be my father. So I had to figure out ways of subduing that kind of relationship that I seemed to be running into all the time.

"Here's what would happen. One of the agents would come over and start putting his arm around me and kissing me and I would just want to disappear into the earth, I was so embarrassed. Like a lot of women, I thought that in some way it was my fault. I knew then, right from the beginning, that I did not want men attracted to me unless I was attracted to them.

"Well, all this went on for a long time. One day, I don't know why and maybe I did it unconsciously as a protective mechanism, I started behaving the way I thought my mother might, and I saw myself take on a kind of protective coating. It worked. I began to feel very easy, acting like their mother. It didn't matter what age the men were. I worked at that agency a long time, until I was twenty-two, and the men could be thirty-four or forty-four or fifty-four and I could still play their mother.

"I learned that if I behaved like a mother, I could be friends with them and they would leave me alone. So, as I got other jobs, I applied the same lessons I had learned in the first one. I started asking my bosses about their problems and work, and trying to help solve those problems, and in the process I was getting ahead because I was making my bosses look good. I was succeeding at work and they were not bothering me sexually.

"After I took some cooking lessons and really got to be an expert at Peking duck, I started inviting my bosses and their wives for dinner and that worked beautifully, too. Because you cook for a man, and I tell you, he really thinks you're his mother."

Five years ago Harriet was put in charge of an advertising campaign for a college development office. The director who hired her was thirty-nine, only three years younger than she was. He was just divorced and coming on strong.

Harriet was, and is, happily married. For yet another time in her working life, she tried the mother ploy. As she discussed it, she idly toyed with her new electric stapler that matched the pencil sharpener. Both in chrome and butter-gold, I noticed. Harriet is a class act.

"When Nick and I would have lunch together in those days, he wanted to talk about his divorce and the custody arrangements for his two sons. I would make some general comments and try to be helpful. I made it clear that I loved Roy and that I had a good marriage and I would talk about some of my earlier problems—and solutions to them —in a general way.

"Nick was interested in cooking and so I steered a lot of our conversations at lunch to sauces and herbs and wines, and began inviting him and his current girlfriend out to the house to meet my family.

"Nick still thinks of me as a mother. The main thing is that mothers are always interested in problems and how to solve them. That's what I've done with all my bosses, including the ones I have now. I am no threat to their wives. I am the mother and I like being the mother.

"Everyone is trying to be comfortable with sex. I can't stand not to be close to the people I like, and not to be friends with the people I work with. But I have to put the sex issue to rest once and for all, so they don't ever take things wrong. And they do respond to my mothering. I'm always listening to the problems they have with their wives and their jobs."

(Yet women executives must be careful not to overdo this motherly concern, as Rachel found out last summer. For four grueling weeks Rachel, a twenty-seven-year-old systems analyst, trained Alex, her vacation replacement on a "temporary" assignment to her department. Trained him? She taught him everything she knew—and more. And lived to regret it. "I made it so easy for him. I gave him a little instruction, step by step, until I made sure he knew it all perfectly. My instincts were to be nice, to be as helpful as possible. How could I have ever foreseen that he would do the job so well that he would get my job and I would be transferred when I got back?")

Typical of the women I see as dynamic "breakthrough mothers" is Gonnie McClung Siegel of Bedford, New York, a communications consultant who develops career seminars for Fortune 500 firms and is the author of *Sales: The Fast Track for Women* (Macmillan, 1982) and other career books.

Active in the women's movement since the early 1970s, Ms. Siegel finds great satisfaction in being a temporary "mother" to young career women by encouraging them to aim for the top but, more than anything else, to become financially independent. "It means so much to them to have an older feminist approve of them," she said, "because they have gotten so much condemnation lately for not carrying their own weight in the women's rights movement and not being appreciative to those of us who opened all the doors.

"I disagree with all this. They are doing the number one thing that will further women most, and that is to be successful in their own careers. They don't have to knock down the doors that we did. They have new worlds to conquer. I believe that earning money and being self-sufficient will further women more than anything else. The moment that women become self-sufficient, they also become independent in many other ways."

I asked Ms. Siegel if she had noticed any different feelings within herself about "mothering" young women and young men.

"It's slightly different," she replied. "In being a mother to young men, I'm always trying to get them to understand the difficulties that young women are having. If they have certain sexist expectations of women, I have no patience with them and I warn them that they are going to have lots of problems if they don't get rid of those expectations."

She drew a sharp line between her kind of "mothering" and the traditional wife-mommy kind. "Other women play the role of mother doing menial chores, like bringing in the coffee. That's not what I consider being a mother. Why, they would even press the man's suit if he would take it off. I see them acting like the cook and chauffeur, which I don't want to be."

Jean, the vice-president on Wall Street who has recreated herself as her own mother, also sees herself as the new breed of office mother. "I don't supply cookies and milk," she emphasized. "But I see part of my job as taking care of people, protecting them from the boss or the boss's wrath, making sure they look good, and that their work gets the best presentation it can. I see my job as training them, teaching them, helping them grow. I feel that I'm growing people. That's my job.

"I have men who are older than I am working for me and I have men who are younger; women who are older and women who are younger. They are all very individual and I find that I have to treat them that way. I can't just adopt a particular style and use it for everybody. I would assume that if you have children, you can't treat them all the same way. For me, it shifts back and forth, seeing them as children, and seeing them as colleagues."

Employees in smaller corporations and businesses owned by women can feel a double whammy: Their Big Mama-owner mother (1) assumes too much responsibility for them and (2) holds them on too tight a leash.

We've all observed these situations in a beauty shop or sportswear boutique or gift store owned by a woman. Once I asked Kate, who owns a jewelry shop and constantly complains about people "goofing off" on her, why she didn't consider some kind of profit sharing to give her seven employees a stake in the operations. "But there *are* no profits right now," she answered. "Of course, I couldn't let them know that because they would get too depressed and might quit. I have to protect them, for their own good. But at the same time, I have to make them work and make it clear that I am the boss."

I think this is tragic for her and for the people who work for her. It defeats her own purpose of making more money and reduces her employees to incompetent children, incapable of understanding the adult realities of business.

Attitudes like Kate's are not confined to owners of small businesses. They are often held by newly promoted women who have replaced a "father" who has been promoted to a higher level. The new "mothers" are terrified at the awesome responsibility of being "the first woman in this position" and they are convinced they must be even tougher than the "father" to keep the children "in line," in order to prove that they are as good as the men they replaced.

The last type of mother is the most difficult of all to discuss because the subject is so discouraging and the situation is often so hopeless. She is the unwilling mother, the woman in her forties or fifties reporting to a younger boss who is intimidated by her track record.

A woman's age, of course, threatens both men and women, although few women executives have needed to react to the threat of an older, more experienced and knowledgeable woman subordinate.

For the present the problem of the unwilling mother is the problem of a relationship between a younger male executive and an older woman—although the man may be only a year or two younger. (In some cases, this issue arises when the man is the woman's age.) He sees her not as an individual but as a "mother presence" ready to scold him, threaten him, punish him, and in every way diminish his authority in front of his bosses and employees.

I asked several management consultants for their advice and they told me the problem was virtually insoluble. "She should just leave and get a job somewhere else," one said.

"She can't win in a situation like that, with a younger boss eager to prove himself. She is just an older woman kind of hanging on," said another.

A third was even more explicit. "A man of thirty-five could see a woman of forty-five or any older woman as his mother. I personally could more readily accept a mother figure if she were more expert in her area and I wanted to go to her for knowledge. If I am her boss, she's got to learn that she's got to use her expertise to make me look good. It's the same thing a son would do."

But a son is not a mother. The expectations are different. To a young man, a son represents promise. A mother represents—well, what are we dealing with here—broken promises? A woman whose boss sees her as a symbolic mother is in a no-win situation. The only way out is out.

The dirty little secret of corporate life, as in real life, is that some men hate their mothers. Some men feel uncomfortable, some feel guilty, and some just resent having anyone around the office who reminds them of their mother.

Yet as long as a woman remains in an office where mothers are welcome, especially temporary mothers, the time-and-again-but-not-forever mothers, she is safe.

I think that the modern breakthrough mother role, if played judiciously, offers several advantages—always depending on the other players, of course.

With the right people at the right time, modern office mothers can dampen a potentially damaging sexual brush with a boss; they can smoothly establish equality and even superiority when they supervise older and younger employees; they can show young men and young women strategies and skills for corporate success, and they can forge essential bonds with younger women on the way up.

Working well with other people, having their best interests at heart as well as the corporation's, works to everyone's advantage.

Without immersing herself totally in the character, the new breakthrough corporate mother promotes herself when she promotes the welfare of her subordinates, when she thinks of herself "growing people," as Jean put it.

Acting wisely and generously, a modern mother can be a leading lady in the office for years. Especially if she gives up the need to be needed, and the need to control, and instead becomes a trusted older friend to the "children" who once leaned on her.

Of course the "children" must be mature enough to allow that transition and not automatically link any older women into their distorted concept of a mother. If they do, she must leave or create another family relationship.

Every day, we get older. A woman at work is penalized more for aging than a man is. Could she avoid the stereotypes of "mother" by acting like an older sister?

SIX

Brothers and Sisters:
Special Ties

"If you follow a man around in an organization, he will tend to see his female peer as a sister and his male peer as a brother. When he looks at his female peer as sister, it's certainly at a different level."
—DR. MARK LIPTON, *psychologist*

Becoming a sister, I once assumed, would be the healthiest of all office roles. A sister would escape the dependency inherent in the traditional roles of wife-mommy or daughter. She would achieve equality, individuality, respect.

This would be especially true in the relationship of women to male bosses their own age, slightly older or slightly younger—men not old enough or powerful enough to be father figures. Most men have less emotional investment in their sisters than they do in their mothers, wives, or lovers.

Best of all, I concluded, being a sister was the closest a woman might come to being a friend and a peer with the men her age. And how about women executives? With them a "sister" might escape some of the ministrations of the smothering office mother who wants to dominate other women. In the same way, for men, assuming the "brother" role might tame the attention lavished on them by an office mother.

Like many theories, mine turned out to have some holes in it. With neither a sister nor a brother, I had idealized a relationship that was far from ideal for most people. They quickly set me straight. If they were the youngest in the family, to this day they remained jealous of the attention and privileges of older brothers and sisters.

First children (especially daughters) resented the responsibility they were forced to assume for younger siblings. Brothers (older and younger) recalled bitter rivalries and, occasionally, bloody fights. Sisters recalled being admonished to "be good" while their brothers were urged to "be smart."

Brothers recalled the anxiety of intense competition with sisters. Whether it was sports or schoolwork, a boy was supposed to do it better. To be bested by a girl—especially your *sister*—was humiliating.

The adults who shared these childhood emotions of brothers and sisters were also convinced that they were never the favorites in their families. Their parents, they said, had loved another sibling best of all. For me, the greatest irony was their wish—*still*—to be the only child!

So the sibling relationship was far more complicated than I had dreamed and, as I was to read, far more significant in child development. "Only second in importance to the attitude of the child toward its parents are its relations to its brothers and sisters," says Dr. J. C. Flügel in *The Psychoanalytic Study of the Family.* Hate, according to Dr. Flügel, is in most cases "the primary reaction of children to brothers and sisters because they must share parental affection and material possessions. Younger children resent the privileges of the older while the older ones look on new arrivals as intruders."

Although jealousy and hatred are usually the first reactions of siblings to each other, in a few years brothers and sisters often come to love each other, says Dr. Flügel. This love occurs usually between siblings with wide differences in ages "so that interests and desires no longer conflict and overlap to the same extent as they do in the case of children of approximately the same age."

From my idealized point of view as an only child, I had failed to fully appreciate the inherent inequality between siblings, society's different expectations for boys and girls, and the critical ways that age and birth order define the feelings of brothers and sisters for each other.

Meanwhile, my interviews were teaching me how people translate these conflicts and emotions into office behavior.

I first met Louisa, a technical writer for a computer graphics firm, at a Midtown exercise class where we were both tugging on basic black leotards. We exchanged stories during the next few sessions, and one day I confided that I always regretted not having any brothers or sisters. Louisa gave me a strange, pained look.

"I'm the oldest of four children, but the only one with a really good job," she began. "I have two beautiful sisters, and my father was not as attracted to me as he was to them. Anyway, I guess that the oldest child is a very special child, a real achiever. I always wanted to please my parents, even though I wasn't as pretty as the others.

"I think there was great rivalry with the sister next to me. I was closer, and still am, to my younger sister, the baby of the family. My brother was the favorite. I hated him. Still do. I was—and am—smarter than he, but my parents didn't recognize it. Well, I make more money than he does now."

As we walked down the steps after class, Louisa volunteered the information that her "strong" feelings about her sisters and brother still influence her feelings about the people in her office.

"I think that on a subtle level I feel some rivalry with the men around me at work who are old enough to be my brothers. Mainly, I just ignore them—the way I do my own brother, whom I haven't seen in four years. As far as sisters go, I've hired a couple of women and I find myself in a kind of rivalry with them that I have to watch because I think I'm recreating something I have with my own sisters. These women are good people, but I find that I don't spend as much time with them as I do the young men, whom I think of as my sons, not brothers.

"The 'sons' come to see me more often, and need me more. The women tend to be very self-sufficient and strong; they are doing well and sometimes I've been jealous of them, especially if the boss goes directly to them, and not to me first. Or if he's just kind of kibitzing with them. I haven't shown jealousy of the 'sisters,' but I have acknowledged it to myself."

The oldest child is often "a very special child, a real achiever," as Louisa pointed out. And, as researchers know, female executives tend to be the first child or the only child.

In many families, though, the oldest sister becomes the "little mother" at home and assumes the same role at work. Irene, a bookkeeper, was raised with the nickname of "Sister Girl" in her Irish Catholic family. She is still playing "Sister Girl" behind the desk she has had for twelve years in the business office of a university hospital in Boston.

"I smooth things out, make everything all right, talk to the administrator on behalf of everybody in the department," said Irene, drinking tea in the hospital's cafeteria basement. "I am the strong older sister who can handle the father and is not afraid of him, because I know that his anger blows over in about five minutes. But he loves to destroy young people who don't know that."

Her office is almost a duplicate of the home she knew for so long in Boston, where she very early became the mediator between her parents and kept the peace among her younger brother and two sisters.

"In this office the 'mother,' our supervisor, is weak and frightened of the 'daddy,' the administrator. He is hateful, vindictive, and comes in often to scold us or to give us more work."

A man of thirty-four reminds her of her younger brother, Kevin. "Fred, the accountant, is our office brat, the pet, and momma's boy, just like Kevin was. Fred tries to get our supervisor's attention and her approval in all sorts of ways, from coming in late to staying late. She thinks he is adorable, even when he provokes her, but especially when he amuses her with a joke. When she does get angry with him, he can't stand it and runs to the three 'big sisters' in the office for consolation. We give it to him to keep the peace.

"I guess I try to keep people happy as much as I can. When I was first hired here, everybody was very competitive and crazy and even locked up their Rolodexes at night. No one would share any information. I started out being very helpful, and pretty soon I got them cooperating with each other, even taking messages for the person at the next desk."

Far from always encouraging equality, as I had naively assumed, the sister role can weaken a woman's credibility. In perpetuating her function as surrogate mother and sympathetic listener, it can prevent her from becoming a colleague of the men around her.

So what is a woman to do? In the opinion of psychologist Mark Lipton, she could become more like a man. He raised that possibility in an interview at The New School, where he teaches.

"Given where we are culturally in organizations and in society, women could play more of a role as a brother," he said. "A brother is certainly a more advantageous role than a sister. If you follow a man around in an organization, he will tend to see his female peer as a sister and his male peer as a brother. When he looks at his female peer as sister, it's certainly at a different level. It's 'I can cry on your shoulder,' or 'You can hold the gossip,' or 'It's easier to talk to you because you're more sensitive.' But when it comes to work roles, to task-oriented roles, these men do not share the work with their 'sisters.'"

"How could a woman be a brother?" I pressed.

"The simplest thing is that she can act like a man. She won't be perceived as a woman and she won't be perceived as a sister. But she may be perceived as a brother—or she may be perceived simply as a bitch.

"I'm not saying women should do this but what we're finding in research is that the women who are winning tend to look like men— tall or medium build, short dark hair, and a nonflattering pinstriped suit. They look like a man and act like a man."

Dr. Lipton had just finished a six-month research project on "homosexual reproduction," the term Rosabeth Moss Kanter uses in *Men and Women of the Corporation* (Basic Books, 1977) to define the practice of bosses replicating themselves at work.

"When a man hires another man," Dr. Lipton continued, "he will try to find someone from the same background, same sports, same branch of service. When a woman is faced with being hired or promoted by a man, what can she replicate that is similar to a man? I was having trouble in my research thinking of what those things could be until I came upon a reproducible characteristic—the same characteristic her boss may possess: Type A behavior—being hard-driven, achievement-oriented, and obsessed with time—the characteristics that the corporations in this country reinforce and reward."

Yet people with Type A behavior stand up to a seven times greater chance of coronary heart disease. Nevertheless, Dr. Lipton insists that this type of cloning is inevitable in the modern office, and it is the price women must pay for success.

"Some people believe that a boss will tend to hire people with supplementary skills, to fill in the void where he does not have the strength. I just don't buy it. Overall, the tendency is for people to look for others like themselves. Organizations are basically masculine. For a woman to make it, she's going to somehow have to be masculine. Now maybe she can look masculine, and behave in a masculine way. One way of behaving is this Type A behavior—aggressive, competitive, hostile, never relaxing, always productive. But if the women who make it are Type A, we're going to have a lot of sick women."

Dr. Lipton's research project involved thirty men and thirty women, all managers at the vice-president level in a large commercial bank. More Type A women were found among the bank executives than are found in the general population of women. At the highest executive levels at the bank, the women tended to look like men—"more tall than short, more masculine than feminine," in Dr. Lipton's words.

He has concluded that Type A behavior may be necessary to reach upper management. However, these Type A women failed to handle stress as effectively as their male counterparts. Women in general, he noted, tend to take fewer sick days than men do. They simply don't see the sick role as an option for them, the way it is for men.

The idea of sisterhood at work was still enormously appealing to me, and I refused to give up my obsession with it. Surely the role could serve an important purpose, despite the stereotypes of the "little mother" that hurt some women.

By now it was clear that sister-brother dynamics are enduringly complicated—more than I had ever imagined. As a child I had pictured an older brother who would find me exciting and amusing, and who would bring home boys for me. This terrific brother would treat me like an equal, respecting me, admiring me, yes, even adoring me. An impossible order, but sometimes we dream big.

Now not only did I have this imaginary wonderful brother, but also a perfect younger sister who followed me everywhere, took my advice, and was even grateful for it. Off and on, depending on how I felt about female authority (and if I were arguing with the female teachers at my all-girls school), I would conjure up an older sister who was not bossy, just worldly wise and loving to me.

As for a younger brother, it never dawned on me that I could be older than a boy, a man. I know that sounds crazy now, but then I thought of all boys as older. I couldn't picture them as being smaller or younger.

These fantasy siblings came alive for me in an office situation (although they were not as perfect in the flesh as in my head) from that first newspaper in Memphis and even after I married, had children, and observed siblings at close range. I look back now and think of brothers and sisters at newspapers and ad agencies I worked for in Memphis, South Carolina, Tokyo, Westchester County, New York City. I remember the help they gave me and the help I gave them and I am convinced again that the sister relationship is a healthy one, with the most potential for equality. But do I think that because I was an only child, free to develop the perfect sibling relationships to suit my emotional needs?

Four distinct sibling relationships exist, each with its special advantages, disadvantages, hidden agendas, and possibilities for competition and cooperation. For women they are sister-sister and sister-brother; for men, brother-sister and brother-brother. The kind of sibling relationships we create, and the success or failure of each (at home and at work), partially depend on age, sex, and birth order. Of the three, I think the most important may be the great X factor of placement— firstborn, middle child, baby of the family, or in between the others.

But in addition, our sibling relationships at work depend on the way a family has helped mold the clay of each personality, determining whether a child will be bullied or celebrated, encouraged to compete or to cooperate.

All these experiences with brothers and sisters are stored forever in our memory banks, to be unlocked consciously or unconsciously in the office.

Playing the role of sister or brother involves us in other people's childhoods, too. The experiences of siblings are different in each family, and subject to surprise scenarios. As we change our own roles and the way others perceive us, so can we help others change the way they see themselves in relation to us. For example, you might even be able to play sister to your office father and get him to see himself as a brother and not a father. Think what a difference that could make in your working life!

To be a sister to another woman without actually having had a sister of your own may be awkward. It could, I suppose, feel even more awkward to try to be a sister to an office "brother" without having grown up with a real brother.

Yet I was comfortable many years in the role of sister—knowing nothing of being a sister except in my imagination. We learn from observation, from our experiences and those of others, and we create the possibilities and the realities from the impossible dreams.

Playing the adult sister has other advantages. It may dampen sexual fires even faster than playing the mother, and it is more natural if the age gap is not too great.

It is also less risky professionally. Consider the role options in a woman's day-to-day office relationship with men. She can be the little girl they protect, the older daughter they teach, the wife they take for granted, the mother they remember with conflicting emotions, the lover they want—or a sister they respect as colleague and friend. Even if they thought of their real sister as "Little Mother" or "Baby Sister," she does not occupy the same place in their hearts as mother or daughter—and consequently it is easier to change their image of sister.

In an extraordinary piece of luck while I was studying the brother-sister possibilities at work, I was introduced to Murray and his unorthodox but highly successful style of operating a business. Murray is only twenty-seven years old, but for the past three years he has been partner in a thriving clothing design firm on Seventh Avenue in Manhattan's garment district. He and his five equally young partners have deliberately created peer relationships among themselves and their employees.

"That's the way we work it around here," Murray boasted, then quickly motioned for silence as he picked up the phone. For the next ten minutes he negotiated delivery dates for quilted storm jackets from Hong Kong.

When we resumed our conversation, Murray wanted to make one "confession": Looking at partners and employees as "brothers" and "sisters" was easier with no brothers or sisters at home. "Well, I do have one brother," Murray said, "but he's seven years older than I am, so I'm really more like an only child. Therefore, I don't go into any situations at work with negative feelings about brothers or sisters.

"Here," he said, "you have a family group, a bunch of friends like brothers and sisters, all working for the same goals."

Alan, thirty-one, is Murray's major partner. The others are Ginny, thirty-one, Bernard, twenty-nine, and Amy, twenty-four. From the start, they decided they wanted to foster a family atmosphere of equals, structuring their firm as completely different as possible from the usual family-owned, rigid, autocratic Seventh Avenue garment house.

Murray knew that kind of place all too well, for he had worked in one for the past two years. It taught him that he could not work for tyrants, nor endure hostility for days on end. "You had six principal owners there, either brothers or in-laws, first, second, and third generations of their families in that firm. I came in with new ideas, wanting to increase profits, but they wanted to do things the way they had always been done.

"There was just too much conflict. Anything I wanted to do, the owners would remind me that I was young and supposedly didn't know anything about overhead, or pricing, style, suppliers, or anything else. We young ones didn't know what we were doing, so we always had to do it the old way. I was treated like a kid and I resented it highly.

"One of the older principals of the firm used to say to me, 'Murray, you can't do it that way. I want it done this way. I'm your boss. I'm the major stockholder with the title.'

"I think that having a relative in the corporation telling you to do something is not like having a boss in a nonfamily corporation telling you. There is much more discussion to it then."

After two years Murray decided enough was enough and announced that he was leaving. That sent shock tremors through the firm. In four generations no one had ever dared say that.

"They told me that I was part of the family and the business was mine, ready to be handed to me if I wanted it," Murray said. "And if not, why not? But you know, it's heartaches there; that's what's handed to you. When I left they felt that I walked out and abandoned them. They told me that I had so much already set up for me. After I left they didn't talk to me for a year. Even now their feelings are still hurt."

Murray and his partners have worked to build a new type of family firm—with friends as family. Although he majored in psychology and has done advanced work in math and statistics, Murray sounds like a management professor as he articulates a complete, well-thought-out philosophy of business. He sees his way of working, his organizational structure, and his attitudes toward women and personal fulfillment as harbingers of the future.

"The old men who run companies like the one I left feel that the woman belongs at home because she doesn't have a business head. If one woman does come into the business, they would never want to be partners with her.

"Now we disagree with that old-school thinking that women belong at home, or else maybe in the factory as workers. We two men feel that our female partners can offer so much more than someone else could. They are equal to us, and we want to stay that way."

Murray fingered a sample turtle-necked sweater (the spring hit that had brought the firm a tidy profit in the thousands) and told me, "You know, in this business, if you're not successful the first year, the second year never comes around."

Why were he and his partners so successful right from that first year? Murray credits their organization style and their emotional maturity. Their young firm quickly won the respect of bankers, lawyers, suppliers, manufacturers, and buyers, he proudly pointed out.

"Nobody assumes the role of mother or father here when we are dealing with people who are older than we are. You have the older brother, my partner, and the younger brother, me. You have another older brother, an older sister, and a younger sister. One reason the sister role is so equal here is that we are all about the same age. If one of the women were fifty-four, or I guess if one of the men were fifty-four, and the others much younger, we might run into problems.

"Before anybody here makes a decision, there is more discussion than there would be in the old-fashioned family firm. For example, finance is my area, and I always look at the numbers before we make any decisions, to see if they balance out to what we need.

"But everything is not discussed all the time with all four partners. If it's your expertise, you handle it—finance, production, design, marketing. But on large matters, there is discussion. If it's something that needs everybody's opinion, we all sit down and talk. We have meetings weekly, and sometimes, daily."

Murray gazed at the display of wool suits and knit dresses hanging on the wall and liked what he saw. I did, too. The skirts were lined, the seams straight, the shoulders fashionably flanged, but not too way-out trendy. We resumed our conversation about how it feels to work in what he called "the square of equality."

It makes you feel, Murray said, as if you are responsible enough to handle your own self, and that feels good. "When you see that you have a successful business, you understand that you've just taken that one step. You've proved your point, and you've proved the point to someone else: that you are *not* a child, that you are an adult, that you *are* growing. Where I was before, in the old family place, they inhibit you and make you step back. Their old cliché is: Wait; you have plenty of time. But in this industry in this day and time it's not the person who sits back and waits who will ever get someplace; it's the person who goes out and achieves."

In a family-owned business, he mused, the stronger brother, the dominating child in the family, would eventually become the dominating power in the business. "Here, if you're a dominating personality and you are used to that and you don't get your way, well, that might be the only clash you might have. We wouldn't put up with it. But that hasn't happened here, yet.

"For me to be dominating, does it make me a better person? Does it make the other person a better person? No, it doesn't. It's what I have succeeded in doing by myself, and what the other person has succeeded in doing that makes us better people. But some men, if they didn't have the dominating decision, would become insecure. They would feel as if they were not needed."

I asked him about the need for a father—his need, and other people's. He saw no need at all. I heard the fear of domination again in his words.

"My father was always at work, and I never saw him. I never felt that I got any fathering from him at all.

"I felt that when I was in the family business, I got too much fathering of a type I didn't want. They dominated me and looked down on me. They would say that I couldn't take orders. So I guess I end up thinking that I don't need a father to succeed."

Then I wondered if he had younger people working for him, younger people that he was bringing along.

"Again, no," Murray replied impatiently. "Again, it works on a basis here where everybody is equal. Our employees—receptionist, secretary, import coordinator, traffic manager—view us as bosses, but again, we don't emphasize that. They talk back to us frequently and we let them ride their own wave. We don't put a strong hand on them, because with that strong hand, you make robots.

"If something in our system is wrong, if something is not working correctly, we want them to tell us, and not to be afraid. If we ask them to do something and they don't do it our way, and it turns out wrong, they have to face up to that. And they do.

"Our accountants and lawyers are in their forties and fifties, but they don't look down on us. We sit together and decisions are made more or less on a group effort. If it doesn't look correct to us, we're not going to do it. We don't take anybody's word but our own. We make our own mistakes."

What would happen if Murray were thirty-five and hired a man twenty-five? Would he play the role of father then?

"Not a father, but again, a brother. I do not want to be a father. Ever. I think that people should stand on their own two feet. I'll help them, but I'm not going to tell them what to do."

How does this new egalitarianism—"the bunch of friends who are like brothers and sisters, working for the same goals"—actually work out in daily office life?

Murray stood up to explain it, walking around the showroom, pointing to his new receptionist. "When a new person is hired, the first thing we do is overextend courtesy to them. We make them feel wanted. It's like a big family opening up its arms, a cousins' club, you might say, bringing them within the corporation, working them in so they feel easy instead of tight and nervous about making mistakes.

"They make a mistake, it's fine because everybody makes mistakes in the beginning. But as they go into the second and third week, mistakes seem to dwindle down to almost intangible. People just pick up and take command of their own jobs.

"They volunteer. They move on. They don't just sit there and become stifled by the inability to move on, because there is always something to do. We tell them, 'Just ask and there it is. Always volunteer to do something. Don't just sit back and say that we didn't tell you to do it.' "

"Just a minute," I interrupted. "How did all this get started? Who dreamed it up? Did you take management courses to learn it?"

"No," Murray answered. "It's the working relationship that we five had from the start. None of us ever took a course in management. It's just what we picked up over the years. We had this philosophy individually, I guess, but it became more dominant when we brought the company together. It's the working relationship we had, the friendship, and we saw how it worked with ourselves. Each of us, that's our personality. We don't demand, we don't yell. We don't demean anybody. Sure, harsh words are used sometimes. They are not used, though, to take a person down and bring them down to nothing.

"Without cooperation, you are fighting against yourselves and it's an impossible situation. So in our family of brothers and sisters and cousins, we give them an opportunity to help us and we help them. We're in it together and it works. They have stayed here until nine, ten, eleven at night because we are all striving for the same thing—to be successful. A few times, they have even worked until midnight, then started the next day right at 9 A.M. There was no arguing about being tired or taking the next day off, or coming in after lunch.

"We may be unusual, but we are not unique," he remarked. "We offer shares and percentages to our employees—to whomever we feel is worthwhile. If they want it, they ask for it, and we'll sit down and talk. If the job is one of importance, then we do that. A lot of corporations are offering these shares and percentages, just to keep their better people."

Murray agreed with me that his new egalitarianism worked because everyone in his company is roughly the same age, from twenty-one to thirty-two. Could it work like this with a wider disparity in ages?

With only a fifteen-year gap, yes. "But once you get into the old school, which I would say is people in their late forties and fifties, it wouldn't work at all. You would just have the old school versus the new school."

But someday, inevitably, Murray himself will be "old school" to newer people. What then?

"I will try to stay aware. I will try to stay within the organization, not put myself in a big office, looking down on people. I will try to stay with them and work with them. Also, there will be more pension and profit sharing. You must offer people the opportunity to climb the ladder with you."

Barely twenty-seven, Murray is already planning the rest of his life, including the day when he will stop climbing the ladder and rest on the steps. But not until he acquires a few more companies. With the enthusiasm of the young and instantly successful, he says, "Entrepreneurs don't want to be locked into one business. They want to branch out. In the next five years, among my goals, I'd like to develop two more companies.

"Alan, my major partner, would like to do the same thing, and I think the two women and the other man want to branch out as well. We might go into partnership with other companies on Seventh Avenue, but again, we might not. We need to diversify because this industry is so vulnerable to aspects of our economy."

Like the young women his age who hear their biological clocks ticking after they have established their careers, Murray hears the siren call of marriage and fatherhood now that he has proved himself as an entrepreneur: "In three years I would like to move out of such an active role and just oversee my companies. Alan would like to do the same thing. We want to take time out, get married, buy a house in the country, raise a family, be with them. But that may be five or six years down the road."

This is a new way of looking at life, and a new timetable for male executives—taking some years off to establish a family and grow with them, once the business is established.

"Well, actually, the business runs itself now," Murray said. "It is self-sustaining. We keep up with it day-to-day and everything turns out fine. The old school would say to suppliers and manufacturers who sent queries, 'Wait; be patient; we'll get back to you.' That's not for us. We set up four or five options, depending on the information we get from overseas, and we give them our answers immediately."

Murray ended our talk with his usual confidence: "I hope that we are trendsetters, the wave of the future in American business. I would like to think that we are."

So would I. Yet so many unanswered questions remain. Will cooperation ever triumph over confrontation among employees? Should it? What would happen to businesses if employees lost that competitive edge?

Will women and men of all ages create more egalitarian ways of getting their jobs done? Or will the paternal model of organization prove inevitable as bosses and their employees grow older?

As more women get better jobs, will they want to compete with men or defer to them? Will women compete more with each other than with men?

To ask the questions is to be prepared someday to answer them. For it is always better to know the questions than to have all the answers. Eventually, answers will come.

Traditionally, the sons at work, like the sons at home, are rivals for the affection of the father, and it is only by besting the father at his own game—making more money, buying a bigger car, building a better company—that they can succeed. Traditionally, this competition between sons, and among all men at work, has been fiercer than it has been between men and women (brothers and sisters) or between two women or among several women (sisters).

New entrepreneurs like Murray and new employees who work with people like him may help topple those old ways of doing business. For reasons of logic and passion. First of all, it is more difficult than ever for a young man in his twenties or thirties to surpass, in life-style and in material possessions, his upper-middle-class suburban father who benefited enormously from the economy's takeoff and the low interest rates of the 1950s.

In the 1980s few affluent suburban offspring can hope to have the houses or the life-styles they enjoyed as children—in contrast to their parents, who always expected to live better than *their* parents. Diminished expectations, diminished egos . . . How can the suburban son achieve? By what measure can he and the world consider him a success?

And in what terms is success defined for a young suburban daughter? Do the male standards of money, career, and status apply to her? Does she marry these standards or acquire them on her own? Must she outshine her mother's professional and business reputation, or her father's? When sisters are raised more equally than ever before with their brothers, will they have the same expectations and opportunities for worldly success? Will the old criteria for success apply to both men and women or will new criteria be created?

Like many suburban, upwardly mobile fathers, Murray's father was "always gone," as he remembers it. That made Murray (1) more independent but more lonely, (2) eager to create a family of friends at work, and (3) determined to find a place and a time to nurture a family at home someday.

Not to repeat the father's mistakes might be one criterion of success —if a negative one—for today's youth. Men like Murray may take a few years off, or even a decade, for marriage and children, to create the family they never had, the family they always wanted—as they create at work the family of brothers and sisters they never had either.

If success is measured in different ways, are personal relationships, too? Perhaps we are moving toward a new idea of family at work, a family of friends, of equals, of brothers and sisters. Rivalry will still exist, of course, but it will be subdued. Equality may be the theme. Is it not better to have a big brother then a father at work with you? Is it not better to be a brother or a sister than a son or a daughter?

Society may begin to see men and women as more alike in their human needs (while still respecting the basic biological differences that create different needs, too). Then brothers will not depend on their sisters at home and at work for comfort in the traditional role-playing, nor will sisters lean on brothers for protection and, at the same time, "mother" them.

If Murray is the future, the new entrepreneurs and their new employees now forging working relationships and life values will define the office family in a brand-new way—as they will define their own families in their own new way.

Murray sees himself as a brother to his male and female business partners and says he feels like an only child because his real brother is seven years older. Like me, Murray idealized a sibling relationship. He made his dream come true by translating it into a coherent philosophy of business management.

True brotherhood and sisterhood, carried to their logical conclusion, would mean feeling deep concern for the welfare of those around you and for the organization itself—precisely the business practice of Murray and his partners. To those who think this is impossible for very long in a competitive, capitalistic society like ours, Murray replies, "Without cooperation, you are fighting among yourselves. It's an impossible situation."

Brothers. Sisters. The young men and women of the new generation feel more equal to each other because they have been raised more equally than any generation of Americans in history. Out of this new equality they may evolve a radically new way of doing business tomorrow—with each other and with the world.

Today, however, most of them are still learning the lessons of sibling rivalry, role reversal, punishment, and other facts of corporate life.

SEVEN

Sibling Rivalries,
Role Reversals

"Think of me as Auntie Mame. That is how I see myself now."
—LINDA

It is 10 A.M. on a day in the life of a corporation. Five men and two women exhibiting varying degrees of anxiety, determination, and ambition enter a room and pull chairs up to a long conference table. They speak quietly, when they speak at all, as they take out neatly typed papers from manila folders. Within seconds an older, obviously important man strides briskly into the room. A quick glance around the assembled group, an even quicker "Good morning," and he glides into the chair at the head of the table. He nods to a younger man on his right: "Okay, let's get right to that problem in the shipping department."

The young man launches into a detailed plan of action, buttressing his arguments with statistics, charts, and the supreme confidence of one who has been chosen to speak first.

"Wait a minute," grumbles another older man slouched in a chair near the opposite end of the table. "We can't go so far out on a limb with this thing. Let's show a little caution and common sense."

Obviously exasperated, the authoritative man in the head chair waves his hand for silence and snarls, "You're dead wrong. Jay has some good points. He makes sense to me, and I've had a lot of years and experience in this business. You've got to be bold here. Remember that you can only jump across an abyss in a single leap!"

This is a typical scene in the corporate ritual known as the planning meeting, a drama played out every day by the stars and understudies of the corporate family.

The authoritative man in the head chair, of course, is the proud, protective father, "the senior man with the broad picture," as management consultants agreed when I asked them to analyze the roles in a planning meeting.

As the father's stand-in, the son makes a presentation to the group. The father knows all the information in the son's speech; indeed, may even have helped write it, but he stays in the background. However, when it is necessary, he steps in to save the son and deflect the attack questions.

The older man who challenged the son's solutions with those attack questions and was immediately rebuffed is the father's sibling rival, his peer in the company. He is still trying to score points, but still losing the round.

When I asked the consultants to interpret the roles in a typical planning meeting, I assumed that the participants would include another challenger at that table—the son's rival and peer.

They were divided. Some told me that the son's sibling rival, the younger, jealous brother, would never even get to the meeting. Others assured me that quite often two young men, bitter enemies, each hoping to be the heir apparent, would cut each other up in front of their "father." But once the father chooses a "favorite son," the losing rival is usually silenced, although he may still attend meetings.

What about the two women? They are viewed as sisters, jealous sisters. "They may be daughters to the father," said one expert, "but to everybody else they are sisters."

Jealous sisters, rival brothers. Out to win.

Why is it that usually we talk "winning" only when we talk sports? That kind of talk is accepted, expected. We seldom brag about killing the competition for grades, for lovers, for college acceptances, then later for jobs, raises, promotions, power—although these are life's main games in our culture, and we know it.

Before we get to the playing fields, the classroom, the bedroom, or the office, we have already practiced winning and losing as children. The home is our earliest competitive arena, and our family members our first opponents. Parents are subtle antagonists for the favor of their children while children fight for the attention of their parents. All children seem to know instinctively how to manipulate one parent against the other. Early in life, brothers and sisters find ways to best each other, to torment the weak and beguile the strong.

At work the people around us become the family members with whom we settle old scores, begin relationships originally denied us, or continue the connections we created so long ago. The same thing is going on for others, too, and we have no idea what springs of memory we are tapping in them. Irrational, unconscious responses between two people or among groups can make them either allies or adversaries on the job.

Once we have a niche—even a temporary one—in the office family and sense the way others fit into theirs, we must negotiate our way through some special situations that grow out of these roles. Much as we may deplore the pressures of sibling rivalries, punishments, rewards, role reversals, and other events in corporate family life, we ignore them at our peril.

In some offices sibling rivalry is played out with the assumption that there is only one basket; everybody must shoot for it, and may the best person win. Not all employees may want the basket, but they all feel compelled to shoot for it, and are diminished in management's eyes if they do not. Competition is heavy but not evil, and management will not allow the winner to harm the loser. In fact, the loser may be protected in some way—perhaps with a new title or a new job to save face.

Running through other offices like an undercurrent is the belief that the person who comes out on top has a stake in the failure of everyone else. All players are not expected to compete, but the victor must knock out the loser—and, if possible, any other challengers.

This is particularly true in the cruelest form of sibling rivalry, one minority against another. Often it will be a black man against a white woman or two black men against each other. Management sets them up, and stands back to watch one fail. It must be either one or the other and nobody else can compete against them. The signal sent by the front office to the other employees is "Let them beat their brains out." Finally, one wins, promotes new people, and sends the loser (and sometimes the loser's friends) farther down the line—by stripping away some previous authority or by ordering transfers to another department. All with management's permission and, in many cases, approval. For no matter which one wins, the company wins. It gets a minority in that position.

Except for some special situations (minorities, for example) management finds no need to set up most people as rivals. Competition comes naturally to those who had siblings at home, and even to "only children" because they had to measure up to cousins and classmates or felt they had to surpass the achievements of one or both parents.

The more you are like your competitor—in age, experience, race, sex, or status—the closer you get to the sibling situation. "And the sibling relationship always has a kicker," says Dr. Muriel Vogel, director of human resources and administration for Lytel, Inc., a New Jersey-based high-technology firm specializing in optoelectronics and the developing and manufacturing of semiconductor devices and computer lasers. She is the former director of research and counseling for The Goodrich & Sherwood Company, a Manhattan human resources management consulting firm.

That "kicker" is one child's impression that the other one got a better deal, regardless of how loving and caring their parents might have tried to be. Usually one sibling in the family (or the class) is not as successful in life as the others are. This often stems from early childhood comparisons ("Cynthia's the pretty one; Cathy is the smart one"); the guilt from not measuring up to parental expectations ("We always hoped you would be a lawyer"), or failing by one's own standards ("I knew I could do better on that examination, but I just didn't study hard enough.")

The intensity of the rivalry we express at work depends on these early experiences at home, says Dr. Vogel. Some parents play off one child against another in a highly charged competitive atmosphere instead of treating them as individuals. When the children become adults, they often feel cheated out of the recognition they feel is due them, and that resentment colors their relationships with colleagues and bosses at work.

Sibling rivalry is played out in thousands of different ways in the business world. The classic good son-bad son rivalry has produced a turbulent effect on the staff of an elegant new California hotel, where Helene has been promotion manager for five years. A few months ago I watched her watching the hotel's general manager, Claude, a lanky, distinguished-looking Frenchman with a devilish mustache, stroll through the cocktail lounge, his eyes periscoping the sexy young things at the bar, the waitresses slithering past the little round tables, the couple in the corner snuggling on a red velvet banquette.

"He's the father here, no doubt about it," Helene declared with obvious admiration in her quiet voice. "He is a commanding presence. He wears those European double-breasted suits and a flowing silk handkerchief in his left pocket. He's an idea person, promotion- and sales-oriented, a natural host.

"Like many fathers, he is not really close to us, but he is inspiring. Four times a year, he gives us a party. He's an onstage, Billy Graham kind of guy, yet he will roll up his sleeves and work with us if we need him. Plus, he always says, 'I want to hear from you what's wrong,' and he means it."

Claude has two "sons" working directly for him in the hotel. He has just promoted one of them to sales director, and Helene and the rest of the staff are puzzled and worried. "This guy is trouble and we all know it. He's rowdy. Doesn't care who knows how much he drinks and how many women he beds down. Even brings them into this bar.

"Nobody likes him. He's a sneaky bastard, demeaning everybody else's operations, trying to make everybody else look lazy, nagging us to follow his directions and doing everything his way. We have learned never to say much to him. Otherwise, it will be twisted to his advantage.

"He's a big showman. He manipulates Claude by flattering him, stroking his ego about his success in taking tourist business away from the older hotels and attracting the convention business of rich professional groups."

The other son, and the sales manager's intense rival to replace Claude someday, is the hotel's executive assistant. "He is not a showman, but a plugger," Helene said. "A real human being. The trusting, trustworthy, dependable one. He freaks out when the bad one asks him why he isn't getting his work done fast enough. But he's too quiet. He knows what's going on, but won't talk about it. He knows we want him to replace Claude, but he's losing out fast.

"As for the rest of us, our sibling rivalry is only with this sales director, and not with each other, the way he would like it to be. We try to ignore him, but it's hard since he's always poking his nose into our offices, measuring us by each other even though our jobs are entirely different and can't be compared. We don't do that with each other. We don't have to disparage each other's departments the way he does in order to get 'Daddy's' love. We hate it when Claude compliments him or sends him off to Europe to study management in one of our other hotels. It keeps us on edge, wondering when he will take over."

Some people, like the hotel's "bad" brother, must try to induce competition among peers even when it is pointless; others impose competition on employees even when it is harmful.

Jerry does this. Jerry owns his own small public relations firm and revels in encouraging cutthroat competition among his staff. His top account executive, Hank, has endured it for eight years. "Competition was always Jerry's fun. He tells everybody that we can all do each other's jobs and write each other's copy. It doesn't matter that I don't know a damn thing about hemlines or that Elaine hates to cook. Jerry wants us all to turn in copy for all the accounts—food, fashion, cars. Then he decides who is best, whose copy is shown to the client.

"Before he started the agency, we were all working other places and we each had our own specialty, our own turf. Now we are thrown off balance. Jerry tells us it is so good to do this, that it reveals hidden talents and makes us grow. I think he just wants to stir us all up, and keep the pot churning.

"Most of us fear him—and each other, as well. We're writing and looking over our shoulders, wondering if somebody else writes it better, will that writer get the account, and will we be out of a job? We're starting to hate each other and to figure out how we can torpedo somebody's idea before ours is down. It's no way to work.

"Susan is the one exception to the fear. She is the baby in the office and throws tantrums, believe me, when somebody comes up with another way of saying something or the art director wants to change her copy. Jerry storms out and asks, 'Now what am I going to do with you?' Just like a father who can't manage a little brat. But she gets away with it."

In a way Susan unites the copywriters and glues the office together because she's such a baby. "A tattletale, too," Hank, the top account executive at the agency, added. "Everybody in the place can know something, but Susan usually won't. For example, one man was in the hospital for a liver problem, and Susan would have loved to run around the office saying how sorry she was for him, and wondering out loud if he had been drinking too much. But we never even let her know about it. We told her he was home with the flu. The more damaging the information, the better she likes it, so we just withhold everything we can from her."

If you get into a malevolent play-to-kill sibling rivalry situation like Jerry imposes, how do you get out of it? Not easily. Usually, it's hard, if not impossible. You either ride with it and do your best, or you withdraw . . . unless you are lucky enough to have a manager who understands and will intervene for you.

A good manager, according to Dr. Vogel, will size up the situation, define what is happening, and help the rivals perceive their responsibilities and rewards. An even better manager will head it off beforehand. "If things are set up on an individual basis, rather than in a competitive way," she explained, "then each person sets his or her own goals and the sibling rivalry will be discouraged."

When colleagues compete for the favors of one person, she continued, so much energy goes into that rivalry that it depletes their energy for the actual completion of the work. Their manager should be alert enough to recognize the problem in its early stages and control it. If that is impossible for your manager or if the manager is imposing the rivalry on you, then the smart thing is to concentrate on your professional goals, save your energy for completing your assignments, and perhaps look for less bruising employment elsewhere.

If your office brother or sister becomes your boss, you may have fewer problems than you would if a new father took over and brought in his own children. In fact, the promotion could be advantageous if you two had a healthy relationship before. You'll have some kind of understanding of your own work habits, the company's expectations, and some knowledge of each other's strengths and weaknesses.

You may consider it a relief that, for the most part, the new relationship is not your responsibility. "The pressure is all on the other person who is now your boss," commented Marianne, a computer programmer hired at the same time with Mark, who just became her supervisor. "He has the cards now. The guy who is put on top after being your peer has to define the relationship. You can't do very much. He has got to be smart and realize how to bring the relationship along. You really can't do anything. You can't suddenly begin bowing and scraping to him."

Yet an inside promotion elevating "one of the boys" or "one of the girls" to a higher rank often implies that a serious contender has lost the game. If you are the one who has lost, management experts like Dr. Vogel advise that you seek an appointment with your boss's boss to review assessments and options. Ask how he or she interprets the meaning of the change and how you will fit into the new structure, saying, for example, "We have had a change here and I would like to know what your expectations are of my job, what my role will be."

If you have lost out in a struggle for a promotion, very often the frustration and resentment build to intolerable levels. You may have to request a transfer or leave.

If you intend to stay, Dr. Vogel recommends that you congratulate the winner and be generous, saying, "I'd like to stay and help you make this successful. How do you see my work within this new structure?"

Reverse the situation and suppose that you become the boss of your former peers. Then it's up to you to set the necessary objectives for the group and for each person. You must quickly communicate your vision of the needs and goals of the department, then ask your subordinates about their needs and goals, their visions of themselves and their work.

One by one, invite them to meet with you. Even better, take each person to lunch. Your message should be "Look, things have changed. I am in charge. The department is my responsibility now. How can we work together to improve things? I see these as your strengths, and this is what you can help me do. Is there anything I have left out? What are your ideas?"

As Marianne correctly pointed out, if you become your sibling's boss, you are the one who must define the relationship and draw its boundaries of friendship and power. Nothing is going to be the same between you. Management consultants suggest keeping some distance and keeping your professional cool. Which makes good sense for any office relationship.

Role reversals involving the promotion of younger and older women over men are often embarrassing and distressing for all concerned. As always, the main way out of the bind, says Dr. Vogel, is to keep your attention focused on the tasks and not the personality.

When a sister is promoted over the brother, or a daughter over a father, or a mother over a son, both of them need to understand typical family attitudes and their own unique family feelings.

Coping can be most difficult when an older woman becomes the boss of a younger man who may project onto her all his preconceptions and experiences (and perhaps, unresolved anxieties) as a son. However, an older woman is not likely to use a younger man as her projection screen because to get where she is she has acquired some professional detachment—after all, she's been in the business world a lot longer than he has.

Dr. Vogel thinks that if a young man has been given respect, responsibility, and a sense of his own manhood without his mother's dictating policy or being overdemanding, he will have few problems working for an older woman. One young man, she noted, praised his boss as "hardworking, smart, no-nonsense," a woman who encouraged his independent judgment. "What she was interested in was only the final product," he said. "How I got there didn't influence her thinking. It's results that counted with her."

Of course, that is the description of any good manager—male or female.

Suppose a woman doesn't want to play the mother role.

To avoid it, she should act like an adult but not a mother, insists management consultant Dr. Samuel Squires, president of Interactive Testing and Training Systems, Inc., and Personnel Management Systems. "It has to be adult to adult," he said, "and she can't slip. She has to watch her communication because she has to understand and expect that these young men are going to look at her as the mother. If she gets into that mother-child communication, she's going to have problems.

"People will treat you according to the way you come across to them," he emphasized. "If you act like an adult and not like somebody's mother, you label it that way and respond as an adult, and they will treat you as an adult. If you respond as a mother, they will treat you like a mother."

Good advice, important advice. But is it always that easy? The skeptic in me surfaced. Sometimes we find it impossible for others to view the person inside us because they cannot see past the mask they have erected between us and our age, our sex, or our race. Their preconceived notions are too strong. Any attempt at change may be a waste of time.

It is not easy to refuse the roles others assign to us and to create the one that is right for us. For eight years Linda struggled to extricate herself from the mother image. She finally succeeded only when she lost fifteen pounds, bought new clothes, switched careers in midlife, peeled off the mother label right from the start, and thought of herself in new ways:

"Friend. Supporter. Helper. Big sister to the younger men and women. Adviser and teammate to the others. Once I thought it was inevitable that you had to be a mother to people ten or more years younger than you. I don't think so now, not at all. You can be a friend. The woman I replaced in this office is twenty years younger than I. She headed the office, and the same men who reported to her now must report to me.

"After I was on the job a week, a young man on the staff whom I had praised for staying late to finish the annual report for the printer came up to my desk and told me that he had an urge to call me 'Mom.' I replied, 'Think of me as Auntie Mame.' Because, really, that is how I see myself now. Not as 'Mom,' a person I used to be, but a freethinking, freewheeling aunt. It is a drag to be the mom and I think it makes a younger man too dependent emotionally on you."

She has good reasons to think so. "My last boss had a need to see me as his mother, even though he was only six years younger than I was. At one point he told me, 'You are always saying I am wrong and telling me what to do. It's as though you are scolding me for doing the wrong thing.'

"I realized that he was right and that was exactly what I was doing. I think he saw me as his nagging mother—and that's the way he needed to see me. When he came to our department to take over, he really didn't know the area he was supposed to know. He began to do all kinds of things that wouldn't work and I tried, in a nice way, to deflect him. But his personal style was so bombastic that he forced me to say, 'No!' rather than allowing me to talk reasonably. And so, of course, I did come off nagging because he made me do it, because I felt that I had to stop him in midstream. After a while he came to rely on my judgment, and I had less recourse to nagging behavior. But I think he always saw me as the mother who kept telling him, 'No!' And I don't want to be that person anymore to anyone."

When a younger woman is promoted over an older man, that upsets our notion of the orderly procession of life events. The daughter bossing the father? "Our society doesn't want that to happen," said Dr. Vogel, "because an older man is supposed to take care of the little girl, so this is a lopsided situation."

Working together productively will be hard for both of them, at first, but with skill and determination, they can do it. First they need to define their mutual professional goals and agree on their individual duties. Doing that lifts them out of the personal and emotional swamp to the higher ground of professional standards and accomplishments.

Dr. Vogel believes that it's not as difficult for both parties when a younger man becomes the boss of an older man. Yet the son's replacing the father at work, like the daughter's replacing the father, reflects society's ambivalence about age. "In many ways we value maturity and in many ways we devalue it," she said. "We value it in saying that you learn from experience, with all the maturity and wisdom that comes from having lived a number of years. And then, on the other hand, we devalue it, by saying that once you're old, you're over the hill, you don't have the energy, you don't have the flexibility, you're not ready to learn. I think that we give very conflicting signals about getting older."

At age thirty-seven Margaret, who had been with the company only four years, was promoted over her supervisor, Ted. He was fifty-four; he had spent the last twenty years running the department and he was counting on one last promotion to sales vice-president (Margaret's new title) before retirement.

"Ted took me under his wing from my first day on the job and taught me the whole operation to make sure I didn't fall on my face when I went to call on prospects," Margaret said. "He's much older than I, and has always liked me. I made him laugh, and we had good times together.

"After that period of learning, he let me take over management of the sales force. Once I had learned all I could, the man who was above both of us promoted me to vice-president. Now Ted had to report to me. I made a deliberate effort not to act like a daughter to him. But some people saw me that way, and maybe he did, too, a little. I tried to keep some distance between us. After my promotion, we stayed good friends—like siblings, I'd say, although I deferred to him as the older brother in some things and the friendship cooled off.

"We continued sort of running the department together. I got all the credit, but he didn't seem to mind too much because he no longer had to report to the top boss, whom he had always despised as ruthless. But I always had to be very careful not to hurt Ted's pride in little things, once I became vice-president. For instance, I always made sure that he kept the best secretary and the biggest corner office."

Deferring to him as the older brother. Being careful not to hurt his pride. Letting him keep the secretary and the office. Women have special role complications in the corporation, which may explain why most of them are stuck in middle management. "Women are still seen as support people," explained Dr. Vogel. "The orientation of our thinking is that the man is in charge and the little woman has the fires going at home so that when he comes home he can unload his problems and she can help him. But nobody talks about the woman coming home to unload her problems and the man having the fires going."

"But now, with new child-rearing patterns, I think that we have a good chance to get out of those old attitudes, as husbands and wives modify their schedules and one spells the other at home, one working late while the other comes home. I'm not talking about the man staying home and cooking. I'm talking about a realistic statement on the part of two adults that they want to have children and they still want to maintain equivalent—not equal—responsibility.

"This will have a profound effect on the sons and daughters of those couples because it will change the structure of American industry. We won't see it for many years. Up until now it's been easier if one of them has been in the arts, or is a college professor, or can work at home. More and more, corporations are recognizing the dual career couple, with things like flexible hours."

Like parents, corporations deal out punishments in different ways. They take away secretaries, titles, bonuses, awards, and plum assignments, giving them to others, along with jackets, pins, raises, and tickets to baseball games in the company's box seats.

Corporations have plenty of other ways to punish, too. You attend the meetings, but your presence is not recognized, nor are you asked to contribute any ideas. Then you are not even invited anymore. Your place at the regular Thursday luncheon is suddenly shifted from the president's right to the purchasing director's left. When memos are distributed, you are no longer sent a copy. If they really want to punish you badly, of course, they exile you to the back room or the boondocks.

Who is likely to be punished? Three types of people, I think: the outdated outcast, the brilliant smart aleck, and the chronic complainer.

The outdated outcast is the person who once stood in medium-to-high favor but is now perceived as too old or too old-fashioned. Maybe this person's biggest sin is just hanging around the place too long. Maybe his/her ideas are too closely identified with managers long departed but long remembered. Maybe he/she derides current management and incessantly compares the present unfavorably to the good old days.

The brilliant smart aleck is the rising star who crashed to earth, the whiz kid with the potential that never materialized. He/she works like a dog, on overtime and days off, coming in early and staying late—and making sure that everyone knows it. Obsessed with his/her own excellence, the brilliant smart aleck cannot suffer fools, and lets everyone know that, too. He/she is a loner who hears only one voice, despises "office politics," refuses to play on the team, and shows disdain and contempt for the captain.

The chronic complainer is the person who needs to be unhappy to be happy, who always has a better way of doing things. Often the outdated outcast and the brilliant smart aleck turn into chronic complainers, a condition which hastens their alienation from the mainstream. Frequently chronic complainers are the worst office gossips, floating rumors that they alone have concocted and which throw the office into turmoil.

Some of these people could be "rehabilitated" into creative and productive employees if managers could bring themselves to discuss the issues and give concrete examples of the behavior changes and work attitudes they expect. Few managers seem to be capable of this.

It is often impossible to fire outdated outcasts, brilliant smart alecks, and chronic complainers. They have union contracts, or they spark the embers of old loyalties in top management, or their boss is a coward who can't handle any controversy—especially personal confrontations. So they are punished in various ways—but most of them never realize that management is signaling its displeasure. They interpret the punishment not as a reaction (which may or may not be justified) to a personal trait, but as one more piece of evidence that the boss is a bum, the company is stupid, and the whole place deserves to sink.

In a family at home one child—or several—may become the scapegoat, a lightning rod for the parents' hostility for a number of reasons: personality, looks, talents, accomplishments, or lack of these.

In the office scapegoating is often a deliberate and effective tool, used more frequently than we realize by management. It is one way to form a group and keep it united, believes Dr. Squires. "A very smart administrator or manager can do that by providing employees with a scapegoat, not necessarily a person, but a competitive company, a product, or a policy.

"I have also seen managers set themselves up as scapegoats to have groups form against them. This is a favorite practice in the services and it is how they achieve discipline. You become the bastard. It happens all the time. And people say, 'Oh, that SOB!' But they do their job, as you can see in the movie *An Officer and a Gentleman,* where the tough drill sergeant who puts you through your paces becomes the sweet guy."

I remember Carl. Who among us could ever forget him? At least three times a week, in a newsroom composed mainly of Southerners and women, he slammed down the phone, put his head in his hands, and moaned loud enough to reach the second row of desks, "Why do they bring me mush-mouths and little girls for reporters?"

His second favorite complaint was that all true professionals stayed overtime until the first edition was up to see if the composing room made any typographical errors in their stories. None of us ever stayed that late, but Carl, who did, never stopped trying to make us feel guilty. He terrorized us and humiliated us. We felt helpless, like children. But he welded us closer than any nice guy ever could have because he provided us with someone to rebel against.

Whether he knew what he was doing or whether he simply had to fulfill the role of scapegoat for his own emotional reasons, I don't know. But he had a searing effect on us. Most of us gave him the best work we have ever given anyone. Sure, we tried to ignore him. Sure, we argued with him, and sure, we usually lost. Some couldn't take it and left. But most of us thought he helped us write the best stories and put out the best paper we ever had.

He demanded nothing of anyone that he did not demand of himself. He came in at 7:30 A.M. and stayed until 9 P.M. He knew how to work the telephones to get every scrap of information for a story and he stayed with his reporters until they did. I have friends who say that he taught them more than anyone else. I was never a fan of his; I recognized his genius in eliciting the best from us, but suffered and endured him in silence. I can understand, though, why he is a legend and a "sweet guy" to my friends. These are the same people who felt that Daddy didn't love them unless he scolded them.

Another type of scapegoat is the Spoiled Brat, as exemplified by Nancy. At the slightest provocation, she runs to the supervisor with her demands—more heat in winter, more air-conditioning in summer. She whines about not closing the office on Lincoln's Birthday and takes personal offense when the entire crew is asked to work overtime once in a while. (She usually wiggles out of it.) Nancy justifies herself this way: "If you make yourself obnoxious, you get what you want, because they don't have the energy to deal with it."

She also leads the office veterans who gang up against a new arrival to turn that person into a temporary scapegoat. "There is a complete closing of the ranks and we ask each other, 'What can we get on this person?' We want to find out why this person left the old job and we get a whole dossier on him," Nancy admits. "We have to know who is coming in to work with us and why. As a new person, you have to make yourself accepted. Nobody goes out of their way to accept you."

Scapegoats and spoiled brats serve several purposes. They are a unifying focus, a convenient target for hostility, a stimulant to office gossip, and certainly a relief from boredom.

In many families three members can sometimes unwittingly form a triangle that excludes the other family members. Before I had children or closely observed other people's children, I assumed that children always united against parents. Not necessarily so. It is more likely that one or two children line up with one or both parents against the other children and the other parent.

The mother and two daughters, the father and two sons, or the parents and one child will form close ties based on special needs (handicaps, illness, talent), similar points of view or personality traits, leaving the rest of the family on the outside looking in. In a family of only three, the bonding of two against one is likely to occur with one parent and child against the other parent.

If we do not work out relationships with significant people in our lives—father or mother or whoever forms that triangle or bond—then these relationships have a way of being played out at work. Hal, a psychotherapist, gave me a personal example. "The triangle in my own family was composed of my mother, my father, and my sister. She had a terrific singing voice, and from the time she could walk, she was my father's favorite. It was a triangle my brothers and I would never understand. Maybe my father saw a great deal of his own status in relation to my sister's success in school musicals.

"I would often observe that triangle because I was outside it. My sister seemed very powerful. She was almost more powerful than my mother. Perhaps for that reason I have always sought out good relationships with women at work. But they never quite turned out to be what I wanted. I think I get them mixed up with the role of that particular woman, my sister.

"At times at work I confuse a relationship with a woman colleague with my relationship to my mother. I seek out advice from her that never works, because she is not my mother, but just a symbol of my mother. I think I do this because my sister played the mother role to me. I didn't go to my mother for advice, or my father. I went to my sister.

"There is some part of my work that produces anxiety. I feel panicky about something and I seek out this female, this surrogate sister-mother, almost indiscriminately, to talk to. It's never worked out. They are never helpful.

"And last year I hired my real sister in this office as my assistant. I felt that I needed to have her around me. But, you know, I never thought about the reasons for all this until this very moment."

Ariel was her father's pet, and they frequently went places without her mother. "I was much closer to my father," she told me. "He is an artist and a creative person and I am, too. We are both Pisces, with our birthdays one day apart. My mother hated anything that was artistic or intellectual and from the time that I was a child she seemed to accept my closeness to him. She would say, 'I don't want to go to the museum, but you and Daddy go.' On the family's only trip out of the country, to Italy, I went with him, not Mother.

"He was my friend. He never was a 'You should; you must' person. It was, 'What do you think, Cookie?' We argued over principles and philosophies every night at the dinner table. And it was always fun, never angry.

"In my first job the man who hired me, the director of international planning, was in every way this same kind of warm, sympathetic, ideal father. I felt like his special person, to the exclusion of everybody else. I was the one person he could really mold and he did. His secretary began to despise me for taking so much of his time."

When we need support at home or at work, we seek out others, hooking ourselves into another person or into a group to get what we think is lacking in our own lives.

What is that missing element? Often a feeling of power, camaraderie, acceptance by the group.

And who among us does not need support? Employees frustrated by their inability to move top management on some issue will form alliances and networks outside their immediate department to achieve a particular goal or develop a special training. We organize into formal groups, like women's caucuses, black caucuses, Hispanic caucuses. When we are members of these minorities at work, we bond ourselves into informal networks based on sex, ethnic affiliation, race, religion. These powerful alliances can transcend titles and status. A black messenger will have access to a black manager that a white messenger will not have.

Often we exclude and include each other on the basis of age, education, and ethnic or geographic origin. (Southerners in a Boston office will usually be friends.)

Who goes to lunch together, who has a beer with the others after hours? Who gets a job, promotion, or raise? That's why management experts advise women and members of minority groups to try to weave some kind of tie of familiarity based on mutual interest (sports, hobbies, children) with a white male boss so they will not seem so "different" to him.

Competition within the original family begins the cycle of networks, alliances, and rivalries that blossom into the complicated relationships of the corporate family. The little boy who felt excluded from the triangle of mother, father, and sister grows up to be the man who depends on strange women for advice, yet acknowledges that "it never works out."

The little girl who went to Italy with her father evokes that "special person" feeling from a male boss who makes her feel competent and comfortable.

Another boy, perhaps excluded as well, failing to get the attention he felt he deserved, compensates by becoming the office scapegoat, the person everyone loves to hate. The baby who threw tantrums grows into the spoiled brat who wants special privileges. That, too, is a way of competing. So is withdrawing and sulking and refusing to play. Or work.

The possibilities are endless. Family members inside the original triangle or twosome may try to duplicate those at the office, sticking together, excluding outsiders, and "spanking" the delinquent. The office wife to the office father may get deep satisfactions from the punishments she helps him administer. The "good" children gang up against the "bad" children.

Alliances, networks, and rivalries are powerful forces within each office. To understand them is to tame them somewhat, to score a triumph by teaming up with the victors and playing the game their way.

Not in every circumstance. Sometimes, to understand them is to admit defeat as the outsider in one situation, with one person or one group, and then to move on.

Just as it was in the family, that place where we first learned to compete, to grow up, to take chances, to lose, and to win.

Eventually, we have to leave.

EIGHT

Leaving the Family:
Divorce and Remarriage

"It feels like a divorce, whether you are fired or whether you choose
to leave."
—ELAINE

Good-bye.

We shut the door on a piece of our life, ourselves. We leave the old
school, the old neighborhood, the old friends, the old routine.

Occasionally, we return—for reunions, weddings, funerals, or simply to wander around, wallow in the nostalgia a bit, and see how time
has transformed the place and our remembrance of it.

I have stopped by that brick apartment house with the screened
porch in Memphis; I have sat again in college classrooms, I have
walked alone down streets of childhood. Yet I have never returned to
any place I worked—with one exception. More than twenty years after
I started work as a teenage girl on that first newspaper, I made a
special trip to visit the new building.

Today I live within a few minutes' drive of several suburban offices where I once worked. I have never returned to any of them. I have exactly the same feeling about the offices I left willingly for better jobs as I do for the offices I left reluctantly because I was laid off in a budget crisis or left bitterly because I quit over professional ethics. It seems to make no difference *why* I left.

The humiliation I still feel at being laid off at one place equals the rage I feel at losing the battle of ideals at another. But I cannot so easily explain my anxiety about returning to the offices where I remember the happy times. Why do I keep such distance from them all?

I am not alone in this deep reluctance to go back to the old office. My friends, too, shut the door for all time, once they walk out the last time. "It feels like a divorce, whether you are fired or whether you choose to leave," says Elaine, an art director who has been divorced once and quit jobs twice. "There's still the break and it hurts. Maybe there's a lot of unresolved anger about problems that didn't work out. And you know that things will never be the same. It is going to be very hard, maybe impossible, to start those relationships up again."

Is it the random, crazy-quilt nature of leaving jobs that makes it so hard on us? Quitting is not a predictable, natural transition in life. Leaving school is. Leaving home for a place of your own is, too. Nice, orderly, normal transitions in everyone's life. But when you leave a job, whether you go voluntarily or whether you are pushed, you know that it was not necessarily in the great preordained scheme of things, but an event that you made happen or one that was forced on you. Either way, it's an event you probably did not anticipate. Neither is a divorce.

But, Elaine challenged me as we delved deeper into the puzzle, isn't it an unwritten law that young people are going to move up, and go on to bigger companies and better jobs?

Five seconds went by. "Sure, but there's no plan for it," she answered her own question. "Nobody tells you that you will be at the company for five years and then you will move on. That is never addressed. But they do talk about the pension plan and the retirement benefits, and all that assumes that you are never going to leave.

"Then, when you do go, there is a certain amount of jealousy on the part of the people you left behind. They are thinking, 'Well, maybe I should go, too,' or asking, 'If this place is so great why isn't she staying? Does she know something that I don't?' or they are berating themselves, 'Why don't I have the gumption to get out?' "

Conflicting emotions erupt all around us when we announce our plans to walk out on the office family. "I always feel envious when people are getting out, even if they don't know yet where they are going," Elaine remarked. "I feel very anxious when they go and I wish they would take me with them. I feel stuck in the job I have now, and I can't imagine where I could possibly go. So when I see other people coming and going, it stirs up a lot of feelings. There's a lot of other discussion when friends in the office announce they are leaving. People will say, 'Oh, she really couldn't make it,' or 'He'll be sorry he left,' or 'He's not going to get anywhere without this company behind him.' "

We want to go out into the larger world and prove ourselves once more, but family is security. We know how they feel about us, how we feel about them. It is hard to let go.

Yet it is also hard to stay behind. Those who are left often feel betrayed and rejected. At the same time, they envy those who are making the break.

A data processing manager who has become a vice-president at forty-three by switching companies about every two years admitted frankly to me, "Even though I have left jobs that I wanted to leave, I have still felt uncomfortable because I knew that the people in that office felt rejected, no matter what the circumstances were. I felt guilty about it. Even though I had a terrific new job offer, when time came to leave, I felt guilty because leaving was viewed as rejection."

Exactly so. "In fact," he went on, "it was rejection. But not of any individuals, just one part of my life. I was looking for a new life. But it was like a divorce." He never returns to the old haunts, either. "Oh, I couldn't do that. It's the guilt and the feelings of rejection. I don't even want to have lunch very often with the old crowd."

The anxiety we feel is also the fear of separation and terror over loss of identity. Many times people will stay married to the wrong partner for years, knowing he or she is the wrong partner, simply because they could neither bear the loneliness nor endure even the temporary fragmentation of self.

In 1984, when the Bell System's twenty-two operating companies were dismantled from the mother company, American Telephone and Telegraph, many of its one million employees spoke in interviews about the devastating "loss of family," calling the breakup "the biggest divorce case in history" and comparing their feelings to the stages of adjustment to divorce or death—shock, anger, disbelief, sadness, and then resignation to the shock. They talked about "the pain," "the sense of loss."

Many of us connect the emotions about leaving a job to those emotions surrounding death and divorce. What we are describing in all three situations is the pain of separation coupled with the loss of identity.

Divorce can hurt even more than death because the death of a marriage is not institutionalized as the death of a person is, says sociologist Jessie Bernard. "The circumstances of divorce do not lend themselves to simple rites of passage which make possible a once-for-all change in personal relations," she writes in the introduction to *Divorce and After,* an analysis of the emotional and social problems of divorce edited by Paul Bohannan, author and professor of anthropology at Northwestern University (Doubleday/Anchor, 1971).

Although divorce is not institutionalized, it does have legal rules and regulations—as we discover when we walk out on a marriage. But there are not many rules and regulations when we walk out on a job. That can make it more painful. We're on our own—with only minimal guidelines like "Give them two weeks notice" or "Try to leave on good terms because you never know when you'll want a reference."

When we leave we want to do it right, but there is no one to tell us exactly how. We have little experience, either personally or with friends, to survive this stressful event.

In *Divorce and After,* Paul Bohannan describes six different crises occurring at the same time during the divorce process: "(1) the emotional divorce, which centers around the problem of the deteriorating marriage; (2) the legal divorce, based on grounds; (3) the economic divorce, which deals with money and property; (4) the co-parental divorce, which deals with custody, single-parent homes, and visitation; (5) the community divorce, surrounding the changes of friends and community that every divorcee experiences, and (6) the psychic divorce, with the problem of regaining individual autonomy."

The same six crises surface during a job divorce. In the first one, the problem of the deteriorating job, you begin to realize that things aren't working anymore. Something has changed, something is missing in the relationship. You feel cheated out of your original hopeful expectations.

You decide to get out. To justify your action, you begin to look around for some "legal" grounds for divorce—which may or may not reflect reality. Two examples: "They're never going to give women (or blacks or Italians or anyone over 40) a fair chance here" and "The new owners are just running this company into the ground."

In the third divorce you size up the money situation. Can you negotiate a better salary in a new job? If not, how much are you willing to settle for just to get out of the present circumstances? Will you trade a smaller salary for more benefits? Will you lose your pension but gain stock options or a better medical plan if you leave? Is it worth it?

Fourth, what will you do about the family you leave behind in the old office? Will your departure mean that your office sons and daughters are left without a protector? Will they be at the mercy of a new, hostile stepfather or stepmother? Will you make arrangements to see them regularly and to counsel them on their careers? Or do you plan to move them with you to the new job?

You must also cope with the reactions of friends and community: "Why are you leaving?" "How can you do this to the company that took you in when you knew nothing and taught you all you know? Don't you have any loyalty?" "Will the new people treat you better?" then—"Can you get me a job there?"

Finally, you must get the psychic divorce—the hardest of all, for it means regaining autonomy. We are often so closely identified not only in other people's minds, but in our own, with one company (like one person) that we cannot break away. Once at a particularly low time in my life, in front of a dear and trusted friend, I broke down. I finally managed to explain that I had been laid off, and without a job I felt as if I had no face. Luckily, I happened to be with one of the wisest, kindest people I will ever know. "Well," gently replied Dr. Raymond Parker, "I think that most of us feel that we are what we do."

I can still hear those words: "We are what we do." I have rolled them over in my brain silently many times, thinking about the implications.

If we are what we do in one job, will we be the same in a new job? Quitting the old for the new means taking on a new face, a new identity. Will anyone recognize us? Will we recognize ourselves?

And if we cannot find another job, if we are forced to do nothing, then we are nothing.

That fear of losing our face, our identity, can hold us in a job long beyond the time when we should have said good-bye. Even long beyond the time we should have quit for good. I have known men in their sixties and seventies who would not retire unless they were promised that a desk would always be waiting for them in the office. I saw several retirees return at least once a week, as a safe harbor, a reaffirmation of their identity.

Author Paul Bohannan believes that the "psychic divorce" to regain autonomy is always the most difficult.

But if we are truly incompatible in a marriage or in a job, we must leave. In many cases we find that we are far better for having done so. For it is a distinctly adult pleasure to discover that though we are what we do, we are also what we have been and what we will be. In leaving the old for the new, we so often find the face that was always there.

Suppose you want to continue a relationship but your company has decided to divorce *you*. In plain English, you are fired.

It is a divorce, all right, but a different kind. Instead of initiating the action, you are the one being rejected. And it hurts even more than it would if you sued for divorce.

Again, you will be involved in the same crises of divorce—this time from another perspective.

If you work for a Fortune 500 firm or a smaller but very progressive organization, the pain and shock of the firing may be mitigated by "outplacement" counseling, which did not exist thirty years ago. Now it is a multimillion-dollar industry.

Today's volatile business climate of takeovers, relocations, mergers, and closings has produced an epidemic of firings, layoffs, buyouts, and early retirements. Outplacement counselors can minimize the trauma of a forced leaving.

The *1984 Directory of Outplacement Firms,* compiled and published by Kennedy & Kennedy, Inc., of Fitzwilliam, New Hampshire, publishers of *Consultants News & Executive Recruiter News,* provides a fascinating inside glimpse into the world of the outplacement counselors and their "terminated executives."

The 1984 directory includes a *Consultants News* interview with William J. Morin, president, director, and chief executive officer of Drake Beam Morin, Inc., the nation's largest outplacement firm.

Most people are fired, Mr. Morin says, because of the "chemical" factor—they cannot get along with their bosses—or the "political" factor—they don't fit the company image or they don't show enough team spirit.

"Of course," he continues, "the lower down in the ranks the person is, the more likely he or she is to be terminated for poor performance, poor attitude, or job elimination. But at the higher levels, it is very much a political or chemical issue. In other words, the individual's personality does not match that of his or her leadership or, more specifically, his or her boss."

Then he reveals another personal, subjective reason why top managers are often fired. It is that old term "a bad reputation," which may hound a capable executive two or three years before he is actually fired.

Usually, his "bad reputation" stems from a social gaffe. Perhaps a man attended a cocktail party where he made a "wrong" comment to his boss or to the company president. The comment might indicate that he lacked "sensitivity" or maybe he just had too much to drink at the party.

Although the man's work might continue to be top-notch, his bosses apparently never forget—or forgive—that first blunder. If he makes one or two other "examples of poor judgments at social activities," he is fired, says Mr. Morin, "and given the reason that he was not performing up to the expectations held for him."

Nearly all Fortune 500 companies use some form of outplacement counseling or job search assistance. This does not mean actually finding people a job, the way a headhunter would, but advising them about their own search. Typically, senior executives get individual attention for several months while others may attend counseling sessions.

Firms provide these services at considerable cost and for good reasons, explains Mr. Morin. First of all, outplacement counseling eliminates the "game" of shelving an executive for several years, which blocks the promotion track for others in the company and puts the man on hold. Outplacement counseling also helps eliminate the potential for lawsuits; helps prevent damage to the company's reputation when it wants to recruit new people or keep old ones. And—if the executive finds another job soon, outplacement helps reduce severance payments.

In his own firm, Mr. Morin says, between 80 percent to 85 percent of the counselees are placed within three to six months. About 50 percent to 70 percent find jobs through personal contacts; about 20 percent find jobs through executive search and placement agencies, and the remaining 10 percent through mailing letters and answering ads. In general, counselees are over forty, with a minimum of ten years in the company, and making $30,000 or over.

"I feel that outplacement will become as large a service as executive search," Mr. Morin concludes. "In fact, when one considers massive layoffs and possible assistance to blue-collar workers as well as exempt and nonexempt, outplacement may usurp the executive search and placement fields in the next decade. One might ask, 'Is this more of the cradle-to-grave for which corporations must bear the cost?' The answer is 'Yes,' and only becomes acceptable when you sit across from a man or woman who has been terminated and see the fear in their faces. Then you know that there must be something done to help these people. Trauma of that nature does not really help anyone, and the havoc it causes on families and on the person in terms of self-confidence simply should not be allowed in today's responsible business community."

In the same 1984 directory, Stephen Cuthrell, senior executive vice-president and director of professional services, and one of the co-founders of Fuchs, Cuthrell & Co., who directed outplacement efforts for the White House staff of President Carter, agrees that business will call for even more help in years ahead: "As outplacement is only one of the human crisis interventions, it is likely that the full-service out-placement firm of the future will be offering a wide range of intervention programs, not just outplacement. Already, many of the firms are offering internal assessment programs for key or questionable management personnel, and preretirement counseling. In later years it is possible that programs covering alcohol and drug abuse, marital situations, psychological problems, and relocation will also be provided."

Today an "outplacement counselor" is often the first person an executive sees after he is fired. (I use "he" because most of them are men, since fewer women hold executive positions.) Usually the first thing the counselor does is take the executive to lunch, allow him to ventilate his anger, and discourage him from suing the firm. After the calm-down and cool-off period, the counselor works with the executive to polish his résumé, take stock of assets and liabilities (personal and professional), improve his appearance by suggesting he lose weight or buy new clothes, and, finally, positions him in the current job market.

None of this comes cheap. The charges usually amount to about $200 an hour, with a $5,000 minimum for counseling and a fee of 15 percent of the annual salary of the old job, plus the company's $1,000 fee. It all adds up to about $10,000 per "terminated" executive. The easiest ones to place are those who are forty years old making over $100,000, and the next easiest, younger executives around age thirty, making $45,000 to $75,000 and willing to relocate.

The most difficult people of all to place are the older men at the top of their corporations, making the top salaries of $300,000 and up.

And they are more vulnerable to feelings of rejection. "Those who have put in a large number of years in one organization will feel that they are cast out, that no one wants them, that there is no place left for them," says Dr. Muriel Vogel, human resources director for Lytel, Inc., and former director of research and counseling for The Goodrich & Sherwood Company. "But as a result of the outplacement process, many of them assess themselves and say, 'I really wasn't very happy there. This should have happened long ago. This gives me an opportunity to take a hard look at myself and do something that I may like better.' "

Younger executives are usually less devastated, naturally, because they are still looking at their future. Nevertheless, getting another job at thirty or forty or fifty depends on the way you project yourself and the talents you have to offer. "It always breaks down to ego and self-esteem, no matter how old you are," Dr. Vogel said.

Attitudes about leaving ultimately depend on the meaning a job holds for each individual. "I've worked with women whose job was their whole life," she told me. "They had no families and their social lives were completely tied up in the job. When they lost it, they were devastated. They lost their family. I've worked with men who felt exactly the same way."

We have two choices when we leave the old job for a new one. We can repeat the same patterns of behavior or we can create new ones. We can continue acting and reacting to people in the relationships that worked for us before, or we can transform our image into a new relationship as a new member of a new corporate family.

Frances chose change. Career change first, then role change. She left a job she had held for ten years—director of a national health organization—to manage a company selling oils, watercolors, and small sculptures by mail order. Her story is one of growth from daughter to sister, a growth that did not occur until she was actually on the new job. While she was preparing to leave, she was still playing the daughter, responsible for the happiness and well-being of colleagues:

"I was determined to be the good girl, and not to leave them in the lurch. I checked around to see who would be my best replacement, picked her, and convinced my boss that she would be perfect. Throughout all the transactions, my big worry was that everyone wouldn't be happy. I didn't want to leave my new executive with someone to report to who would make her uncomfortable. I wanted to leave my boss with a replacement for me who would make him comfortable. And I made it happen for both of them.

"While I was leaving the company and making all these arrangements, I felt as if I were secretly leaving over the wall, like the nun did when she came out of the convent in *The Nun's Story*. When I went into this company, I gave it absolutely everything I had. Everything that was within the spectrum of my moral consciousness. Making the decision to leave was terribly wrenching. I had given everything I had to the women's group, to my department, to the ideal that I was representing in the different philosophies of community service and international exchange of health statistics.

"Leaving meant leaving a large part of myself, of what I had worked for. I had done everything I could to achieve a high-level position as manager and it wasn't all for me. It was because I believed in the organization and what it stood for. Ten years is a large part of your life. It was the way it is when you are leaving the nest for the first time. I'd grown up in there; now it was time for another phase of my life.

"I feel strongly that the whole company was my family. Despite the bad, most of it had been good. Whatever happened, I had nothing to regret because I had given and I had enjoyed giving. I had achieved, and if I had not gotten the recognition and the money I wanted, I didn't blame anybody there. Truly, I think we make our own successes.

"I had gotten boxed in, but I had allowed myself to stay in that box. And the only way I could have gotten out of that box was to say 'No' sooner and to leave sooner. But the bird wasn't ready yet to fly. When I decided I could fly, I did.

"But first I had to make everyone happy at the place I was leaving. I wanted all the knots tied, and everything to be in place—so I could leave with a good conscience. It's just like leaving your home. You want to be sure that Mom has something to do and Dad has something to keep him busy, too. You're not going to leave them out on a limb."

When she left she vowed that this time things would be different because she would be different. "In my new job I could easily still be the daughter with two fathers, since I work directly for two partners who own the company. But, more and more in my new situation, I see it in a different way. Instead of fathers, I see them as brothers. And I think that is terribly healthy for me and for them.

"I see them differently, I guess, because I don't see myself on a lower level than they are. I know I am, of course. I am fulfilling a function which is subordinate to theirs, but in my head I am right where they are. In my head my best help to them can be only if I am on the same level with them—if I advise on the same level, if I think on the same level, and without thinking in fear.

"I intend never again to think in fear, as I did before. And most of the fear that was involved was never fear about what would happen to me. I never minded that. Perhaps I was the bad child of the company for that reason. I always spoke my mind. The day I left I asked a friend, a vice-president, why I hadn't moved forward. She said, 'You're different. You're always too honest. You say what you really think.' That was true. I had set my mind in a patterned way, a logical way, and a destructive way, but nevertheless I always said it and they knew I would. So I hadn't played the right game there.

"In the situation I'm in now, I've got to be me all the way because that's what they need to succeed, and so do I. They need an equal talking to them."

She frowned. "They force you to be one or the other—sister or daughter. And of course that was easy for me to choose. They dare you. They play games of confrontation. You have to come back and say either, 'Yes, I believe this, and you're wrong and I'm right,' or let them say, 'We'll tell her what to do.' I don't want that.

"It feels wonderful to be a sister and not a daughter. Finally, flying. Finally, soloing. I know the whole time that I may be wrong, whatever I stand up for, but I also know without any sense of insecurity that they have been wrong, too, and we're all going to be wrong sometime, and it doesn't make any difference. So I score, so you score. They know that I'm here to do the best job I can for them, and certainly I know that's what they're here to do, but they're going to fail anyway, just as I will, once in a while."

Not enough people are willing to change their perception about themselves. Too many enter a new job as they do a new marriage, repeating the mistakes of the old one. With some kind of formal or informal intervention, or even by themselves, they come to terms with the part they played in the problem—what they did and how they did it. Then they are able to change.

Career counseling frequently helps an employee make the slow transition from Bad Child, Spoiled Brat, Crybaby, or Whiner to a more adult role.

"For instance," said Dr. Vogel, "one woman I worked with was highly critical of things that went on around her and her co-workers. She made things very uncomfortable for herself. She felt that she knew how to do things better than anyone else, and she probably did, but it wasn't getting her any place.

"She was transferred to a new job and was beginning to do the same thing. She realized what she was doing and said, 'Here I go again,' and asked me for help.

"Companies call counselors in when they are having problems with someone, like this woman, who is producing very well in one respect but poorly in another area. We interview the managers, the supervisors, and the individuals with the problems. We talk to them all and we ask, 'What might you have done that would have led you to a different result?'

"The woman I was counseling realized finally that what she was doing didn't work. Now, when she catches herself being overly critical and rude, she has a negative image in her head about that and she stops it. It's the same principle that people use to stop overeating and to stop smoking.

"If you start modifying your behavior and getting some positive feedback, that feedback will reinforce that modification, so that you are more likely to create a positive situation. For example, if you start out a new day by saying, 'Good morning,' you are setting the stage for positive feedback. We tell people, 'It's up to you. You are the actor. You are not the receptor. You can create a positive situation or you can create a negative situation.' "

Barbara learned valuable lessons in her three years with a city planning department where two directors quarreled incessantly over her duties. She learned to challenge them about the conflicts, to articulate her own goals but, most important, to compromise.

A month ago she entered into what she calls "a second marriage" as one of a city manager's top administrators, overseeing a department of fifty people. "We'll start with a courtship, a honeymoon," she said. "They really wanted me because they hired a search firm to come after me. I feel very good about it, excited, anxious, and I'm sure it's all going to work out better this time around. I'm going to take it slowly, day by day. I'm going in expecting to care about the people.

"When I first arrived, I went in and asked for a clarification of what they expected from me, and how they expected me to go about doing the job. And then I told them how I felt and what I wanted. I'll keep checking with them to see if I'm on the right track. We will set up some goals, some guidelines. Then I want to go around and meet people and get familiar with my new home, find out where everything's located, who's who and what's what.

"Then I'll start interviewing, taking notes, seeing how things work, what it will take to do the job. I intend to give it 100 percent. I don't think that working hard ensures that you will get ahead. I find that getting ahead has to do with how you treat people, how you handle your relationships, how you are perceived, how the work that you do is perceived, the public relations work that you do. It's what I call working smarter and not harder.

"I have men who are older than I am working for me and I have men who are younger; women who are older and women who are younger. They are all very individual and I find that I have to treat them that way. I just can't adopt a particular style of interrelating and use it for everybody. Sometimes I see them as my children and sometimes as my parents. I'll ask for information or go to them to have someone to talk to. So it shifts, just as in a marriage, where sometimes I play Big Mommy to my husband and sometimes he plays Big Daddy to me. And sometimes we are adult to adult. I have the same shifting relationships with people I work with. So it is not static."

Being forced at age sixty-five or seventy to leave the company can become a symbolic, and then an actual, death. Fatal heart attacks often follow retirement.

Some retirees cling to the office for years, coming back to sit at an empty desk or pass the time with old friends. Either way, the problem is making the office too much a family. A common current tragedy, one that we must all recognize.

We often cling to the office family too long, past the time we should have struck out on our own. We listen to the people who tell us that a bad marriage is better than no marriage at all. We believe that the grief we know is better than the grief we may find elsewhere.

In most cases a new job is an improvement over the old one. Getting a divorce from the old company and beginning a second marriage with a new one is a painful, frightening, but potentially hopeful and liberating experience. The divorce and the leaving can be the best things that ever happened to us. Of course, we never know that until they do.

Until we know that the face that we finally discover is ours, and it is the face we had all the time.

NINE

Crisis in the Office:
Where Are the Grown-ups?

"I'm tired of bosses who act like little boys."
—MARILYN

"This guy is probably having an early male menopausal identity crisis.
I think he wants to be a son."
—PATRICK

For two years I explored relationships inside the American office of
the 1980s. Men and women at work told me their stories. Management experts told me their theories—then went on to describe their
own encounters with the "family at work."

Eventually almost every conversation returned to one theme: good
management—the lack of it, the need for it, the hunger for it. The
longing for fairness, for leadership, for justice. For simpler, less convo-
luted, more straightforward relationships. For professional cool
warmed by the spirit of generosity and the fair play of a loving family.
Recognition of the often childish and capricious nature of corporate

life and, at the same time, an overwhelming wish for something more rational, civilized, and adult. Realization that role-playing carried too far can hurt and humiliate.

The men and women who confided in me wanted their corporations to recognize them as individuals of unique worth but, at the same time, as members of an interdependent system.

Family relationships at work were inevitable, often valuable, most people acknowledged. But why, they asked, must these relationships degenerate so often into the pathological?

The most frequently voiced complaint was that managers reverted too fast into infantile behavior. They based promotions and raises, hirings and firings almost solely on a candidate's personality as long as he or she had demonstrated minimum competence. Managers used their own highly subjective criteria about personality, grounded in their own ego needs and vulnerable to gross errors in judgment, instead of basing their decisions at least partly on more objective standards of job performance or potential ability.

As Marilyn discovered. Four months out of graduate school with her MBA, Marilyn was hired by an international bank. There she would get another graduate course, this time in management-by-whim. It would work to her advantage one time and to her disadvantage the second. It would also make her forever doubt the sincerity of any promotion policies.

"When I started work on the bank's finance staff," Marilyn told me, "it was clear that we were all the children and I was going to have a great many sisters and brothers there in competition with me. Everyone wanted to become a manager. We knew that we had to help each other at first while we were on the staff, but at some point we would be contending with one another for a management position.

"We were working for this guy who really did cheat us, making us stay late and asking us to do other departments' work without ever giving a bonus or a raise or even thanking us. He always invoked the possible wrath of the top boss. He would spring jobs on us suddenly, saying, 'We've got to get the financial statement finished by the end of this week,' or 'This report has to be out tomorrow.' He was a cold, mean, distant man who was very angry if we didn't do our work in time. He was always testing us, and eager to prove himself in order to get his next promotion."

Marilyn concentrated on being a "good child" in order to get promoted out of the finance department. She did what they had instructed her to do in college, which was exactly what bank executives advise employees: Work hard, work more, work long, and you will be rewarded.

"But the way I finally got off had nothing to do with how it is supposed to be," Marilyn recalled. "They told us to work, work, work, and they would recognize us and move us along. I believed them, and I was staying late, until nine about three nights a week, but my boss never even mentioned it.

"One Friday morning at eleven he suddenly announced that the accruals—expenses to be incurred for which we did not have invoices at that time—were due at 1 P.M. I knew we couldn't possibly get them done on time. So I just gave up.

"I made myself some herb tea, took out my package of sunflower seeds, and I just sat at my desk, not really doing any work, very depressed over my chances of ever getting anywhere. Then I saw this guy walking down the aisle. I smiled at him. He reacted as if he were in shock, like a lonely little kid who just found a playmate. He came over to me and said, 'Do you know I've been with this bank six months and you're the first person to smile at me?'

"I told him to sit down. I shared my sunflower seeds with him and asked him if he wanted some herb tea. He laughed and asked me to lunch. It turned out that he was the controller for the international division. And that's how I got into management. We became really good friends and discovered that we had some things in common, like once owning Labrador retrievers and spending a summer in hostels all over Europe. He offered me a position within his division. Although all the other people on the finance staff were Harvard or Stanford MBAs, and I had my MBA from a local college, I was the first to become an officer and go into management—because I stopped working, smiled at this fellow, and shared my sunflower seeds!

"Although we were friends, he was clearly the leader and I was learning from him. We were about the same age—in fact, he was five months younger. But yet, he was my mentor. After all, he made me an officer. And the international group is very hard to get into. You're supposed to have languages and be at the top of your MBA class from Harvard or Stanford.

"All the time I worked for him, he needed reassurance that I liked him and that he could trust me. He was easy to work for, but I had to keep remembering that he was anxious to be loved and appreciated. I pointed out how successful he had become in so short a time, and how much everybody admired him. After a while, it got to be exhausting. And after a while, I also needed some praise."

Two years later Marilyn was promoted to her present job as the bank officer in charge of buying updated computer software and hardware for all the branches. "Now I'm working for a man who needs someone he can control. He thought I would be easy because I am a woman. He is a dominating, brilliant person who really knows what he is doing, building an empire, and doing it extremely well. But he has to have things his way. He has to be right, and he has to prove that the people around him are wrong. After a while, I realized I could never win with him. And I am never going any farther as long as he is here.

"Fathers—dominating men like this one—have to be in control. And the ones that succeed are very bright. It's almost as if they succeed in spite of themselves. I'm not sure that this controlling, dominating behavior really works. I think what really works is their brilliance and that, in a sense, saves them. My relationship with this boss is that he is clearly the father, and I am a sort of wife. Once, in a kind of Freudian slip, he was talking to another manager and said about me, 'Well, I have to listen to her. She's like my wife.' It was a joke. He doesn't listen to his wife at home, and he never listens to me, either."

Marilyn sees her future advancement blocked by this man's emotional needs. She intends to leave the bank because of him. "He is just using me to feed his ego, to control me. That's why he promoted me in the first place. When I leave, I'm going to try to find a job in a more normal environment—if there is one around. I'm tired of bosses who act like little boys or bosses who must dominate, bosses whose fantasies you have to play into if you want to get promoted, or just keep your job."

As beneficiaries or as victims, we have all felt the consequences of personality on hiring decisions and on office morale.

Eventually, you can reach a point where you are fed up with the role-playing. Patrick has had it. After repeated personality clashes with bosses and subordinates, he left the office one day with severe chest pains. Then he went on sick leave, and finally resigned. After looking for another job several months, he is now being interviewed for a $75,000-a-year post as senior public affairs officer for an oil company. Patrick, slim, vigorous, and a commanding presence at fifty-five, still has all his wavy brown hair, now graying gracefully at the temples. He has been called back three times to talk with the vice-president, a balding, rotund, old-looking forty-nine.

"This guy," Patrick thinks, "is probably having an early male menopausal identity crisis. I think he wants to become a son again, to have his youth back, to find the actualization of his young man's fantasies through a father figure—and he wants to use me as that father figure.

"If I try to deal with him on that level, I am lost. I know because I deliberately chose this course at my last job where I told them, in effect, 'Never fear, Patrick is here and everything will be all right.' And it was. As their father, I listened to everyone's sick fantasy. I had to escape it.

"So now I play games with him as he is interviewing me and try to keep the conversation on a more impersonal track, rather than listening to his troubles. I do not want to become a dump for his neuroses. I want only a business/professional relationship with him, and I may not even want that if he continues to act crazy."

Patrick's long years in corporate public affairs and promotion for department stores and cosmetic companies have convinced him that when people in an office are so entwined in each other's lives, a pitifully small amount of work gets done, much of it inferior. That is only the beginning. All employees suffer when a day in the office begins to resemble a gripe session or a therapy group. For him, the solution is simple, and is similar to Margaret Mead's advice about avoiding corporate incest: People who work together should make a deliberate decision not to get too close to each other.

"Even if you are only a Dutch uncle to a woman, or a younger brother to an older sister—which was the situation for me at the last office I worked in—that means that you're still getting into a very volatile situation that will explode in your face," Patrick said. "I know enough from my personal life about how frightened women can get when they get close to a man after they have had problems with their father, ex-husband, or boyfriend. When that begins to happen in a work situation, it can devastate an entire office."

Despite the difficulties, it is possible to avoid the damaging entanglements, he maintains. "I have been in several situations where people have been grown-ups at work. Crazy grown-ups, crazy relationships, but they clicked. When relationships become overloaded with sublimated reenactments, acting-outs, surrogates, then you've got trouble. Now if I begin to sense the power and ego of someone wanting to be my father, or the early male menopausal identity crisis of someone wanting me to be his father, I don't play into it."

In Patrick's experience an organization often changes employees' personalities. Because most large organizations are "hopelessly sick," he says, its people begin to get sick, too.

"But there can be a happy medium where people function as father and mother, son and daughter to each other, without the undercurrent of irrationality and pathology. What matters most is to be happy in your job with an organization that is doing something you can really relate to, where you can create."

Marilyn and Patrick feel angry, cheated, and frustrated over the personal idiosyncracies—more than that!—the neuroses of bosses and colleagues. Their feelings, shared so widely, point to the most fundamental and critical issue facing corporate management today: the lack of leadership.

As a people we Americans are aware and concerned about the mismanagement of employees and the heavy price we pay for corporate incompetence.

In a three-year study coauthored by Dr. Daniel Yankelovich, the opinion analyst, and reported in *The New York Times,* 61 percent of employees listed "pay tied to performance" as their first priority at work. Yet all around them they saw rewards and recognition given to people doing inferior work. Their obvious conclusion: High quality of work and good performance on the job are not valued the way bosses insist they are.

Only 22 percent of employees interviewed reported a direct connection between their work effort and their paychecks. Only 13 percent felt that they would benefit directly if they worked harder. Only 23 percent said they were working at full capacity.

The "people problem" is a growing problem of international dimensions. Foreign imports have killed or wounded American industrial giants. Our money and technology are useless in saving our country from foreign competition, believes Dr. Yankelovich, and tightening the authority screws on employees will not solve the problems. Instead, his report recommends that companies link employees' pay to performance, encourage employees to help develop work standards, and offer them a share in the gains from productivity.

One executive may have a great idea for productivity, but without support from top management and cooperation from other managers, the idea may be doomed to failure. That may be the lesson to be learned from a new paint plant in Kentucky. With surprising candor, a vice-president of that plant complained in an issue of *Behavioral Sciences Newsletter* that his fellow managers were endangering the chances of workplace innovations like his—which had already doubled the effectiveness of the new plant by cutting operating costs and improving safety, quality, and productivity.

Traditional cautious managerial style threatened his profitable "careful human resource planning"—an attempt to involve workers in their jobs and in decisions that affected their work lives—on the reasonable theory that those closest to the machines may know something about their operation. All the plant's 170 employees were divided into nine teams. Each person learned all the jobs within a team and received more pay for mastering each new job. They were all consulted before important decisions were made by management.

Sounds great, right? But wait. The executive was pessimistic about the chances for "widespread changes in work environments." Too many managers felt insecure about the substantial changes in the work environment. Other managers were impatient for quick fixes. In this company, as in others, top management as well as middle management failed to back up the idea man who proved that his ideas worked.

The Quill, a journal published by Sigma Delta Chi, SPJ (Society of Professional Journalists), reported a startling hypothesis about management in my own field: If newspaper editors shared power with reporters, the whole country would be better off, theorized Michael Maccoby, a psychoanalyst and director of the Harvard Project on Technology, Work and Character, based in Washington, D.C.

Mr. Maccoby called the basic newsroom power structure "very paternalistic" and "hierarchical." As a result of the system, reporters and editors burn out or strike out as loners and cynics. "And I can't prove this," he added, "but I think it affects the way they view the news. They tend to have such a sense of their own powerlessness, but they are around such powerful people all the time. I think it leads them to a desire to knock down the subjects of their coverage. It's a form of displacing their anger. They do to the subjects of the news what they would like to do to their editors."

Newspaper reporters are not the only ones who have become frustrated over their powerlessness in the office. Too many of us work in a twilight zone of chaos and suspicion, our duties and goals ill-defined, our managers free to indulge themselves in personal quirks. We resent the company that tolerates this kind of childish behavior in its executives. They, in turn, treat their subordinates like dopey children—who are then free to act like children.

Some industries are notoriously inept at managing people—notably, publishing, broadcasting, advertising, automobile, banking. In other industries (especially computers and consumer products) a few outstanding firms have well-deserved reputations for managerial excellence—among them, IBM, Digital Equipment Company, Hewlett-Packard, Procter & Gamble, Johnson & Johnson, 3M.

As the voices in this and in previous chapters have revealed, many of us work as children under the direction of children. To make things worse, we work under crushing levels of managerial incompetence and laziness. (I remember reading that a Japanese automobile plant needed only five executives compared to the twelve in a comparable American plant.)

No wonder we have an "authority complex" of fear and hostility in the workplace! No wonder we have stress-related diseases like heart attacks, high blood pressure, alcoholism, ulcers, depression, even cancer, for numerous studies indicate that people with no power to control their decisions and therefore their lives are more likely to develop mental and physical illnesses.

Good corporate management may be rare, but it is not all that mysterious—just note the current flood of "how to" management books and the torrent of workshops on the subject.

Are all the books and counseling reaching the right people? Not unless presidents and chief executive officers are reading and listening. Their involvement is critical, says consultant and psychologist Dr. Samuel Squires. "Look," he emphasized, "any corporation is only as good as its upper management. And that's passed down. It's relatively rare when you have a grassroots movement upward that causes the corporation to change."

His ideal manager is an "adult"—and he kept returning to that description as he detailed the qualities lacking in the typical American manager today.

To Dr. Squires, ideal "adult" managers have the vision to define long-term strategy for the company's people, products, and profits. They motivate employees to work hard. They give credit freely on a job well done. They encourage employees to present new ideas—and they have the experience and wisdom to choose the best ideas and discard the others without making enemies.

Dr. Squires called the family model of management a good one if the office family is a good family where people assume responsibility for their own actions and accept the consequences of attempting to solve their problems. Summing it up, he said, "I would define it as a mature relationship."

But then, I asked, in all these mature relationships, would there still be a mother and father? If all the staff members are adults, what would they be to each other?

"Friends. Firm and fair."

"But friends aren't family, Dr. Squires."

He shook his head. "Well, you can be a father and a friend, a mother and a friend to your children at the same time, can't you? An adult friend? Absolutely."

I yearned to hear some talk of fairness and equality. I was not to hear it the way I had wanted—as a plea that managers first recognize the need for fairness and equality and then incorporate these qualities into their management styles. For life within the corporation, like life outside the corporation, does not run on the wheels of justice.

Dr. Muriel Vogel, human resources director, spelled it out precisely. "I don't believe there is equality in the corporation," she stated. "It seems to me that there are certain values in each corporation—corporate cultures, if you will—and if you adhere to those values, if you are in fact a practitioner and you represent what they value, you will get ahead.

"Two men or two women, equally smart and productive, may not receive the same rewards. It is management's perception of how individuals fit into the corporate culture that influences the decision of who gets rewarded and how much is rewarded. If an individual is unable or unwilling to adapt, that person should seek another environment that is more compatible.

"The corporation is not fair. It would be easier to deal with a situation where a task is defined and rewards are given based on the accomplishment of the task, but many other variables are at play."

Depressing words, distressing words for those of us who want to believe in fair play and fair pay.

Especially for women. They have a particular dilemma here.

Throughout infancy and childhood, a girl is aware that she is like her mother, the first "love object" in life. She is encouraged to identify with her mother and imitate her.

The mother is also the first "love object" in life for a boy, who is not like her; he must not identify with her or imitate her, and, in fact, must separate from her at an early age to establish his own identity as a male.

In infancy and early childhood it is easy for a little girl to assume that the world of home and nursery school is built on feminine values and feminine roles. She quickly learns, however, the reality of a world where to be male is to be normal and to be female is to be deviant from the model by which nearly everything in the universe is judged.

Male values, opinions, and behavior are the norm in adult life. Men wield enormous power over women in business, medicine, law, education, government, psychology, economics—every important field of human endeavor.

And so women enter an unequal corporation more unequal to begin with. Unequal to the stereotypical male executive in looks, life experiences, expectations, attitudes, and especially a female value system which considers relationships among the team members more important than rules of the team.

Women also enter the corporation with another handicap: the assumption that they can, and they will, drop in and drop out at their pleasure. Many people believe that women have the luxury of choice in working; therefore, an enormous advantage over men. There is less pressure on them to succeed at work in order to be loved. If they have a husband, they can always go home and be a wife or raise children as their "career." If they do not have a husband, maybe they will get one and leave.

But no man can be a husband or father as a full-time career and maintain his self-respect. To be loved, he must prove his competence and his manhood in one way: work.

The female role in the family is dependent and the male role is independent. Women at work are often seen as dependent and, at the same time, nurturing; as enjoying options (be beautiful or be smart) while still needing a man's protection; and despite evidence to the contrary, as temporary sojourners in the work force. Naturally, men resent and, at the same time, envy these "advantages."

The pervasive view of women as dependent, optional, and temporary workers continues to slow women's progress.

Just "being a woman" was described as the major obstacle to success in a survey of three hundred senior women executives (mainly vice-presidents; average salary, $92,000; average age, forty-six) by Korn/Ferry International, an executive search firm, and the University of California, Los Angeles, Graduate School of Management.

In this survey, reported in *The Wall Street Journal* by Jennifer Bigham Hull, the women credited their successes to ambition, drive, and a willingness to take risks, and blamed their failures on a male world and their lack of confidence in it.

"Asked whether 'barriers to women have fallen at the senior management level,' 63 percent of the women say 'No,' " Ms. Hull wrote. "And 70 percent say women don't receive equal pay for comparable jobs. Female executives most frequently mention 'being a woman' as their major career obstacle, citing 'the old-boy network,' 'insecure men,' and the attitude that they're 'too good-looking to take seriously . . . will run off and get married' as workplace problems."

Ironically, at a time when mismanagement of employees is so pervasive, research finds that the main defense against stress (including associated ailments like obesity, sexual dysfunction, and depression) is support from one's boss, not support from the family at home. "The findings have strong implications for management styles," reported Daniel Goleman in *The New York Times,* "suggesting that it is not so much the personality of the boss—whether he is a warm or cold person—that matters, as his approach to his subordinates as they struggle to handle their problems." Again, the issues of power and control surfaced. Researchers concluded that good bosses empower their subordinates by trusting them to do their work well and by providing the tools for solving problems but not the actual solutions.

Surveying 170 workers from middle management on up at an Illinois subsidiary of the American Telephone and Telegraph Company before the company's corporate breakup, the researchers discovered they could divide the employees into two groups: Those who were under considerable stress but felt that they had their bosses' support suffered half as much illness in a year as those who believed they did not have that support.

"The researchers observed that some especially resilient workers have a group of traits in common—including a sense of commitment, a feeling of exercising control over their lives, and an enjoyment of challenge," explained Mr. Goleman.

In the same *New York Times* article, Dr. Harry Levinson, psychologist and author, commented, "All organizations repeat the basic family structure. Our earliest experiences with our parents are repeated in our subsequent relationships with authority." In Dr. Levinson's opinion, the best executives are like parents, helping others to grow and develop their abilities.

Children grow up to be competent adults only when parents themselves are adult enough to let go and empower their children with the trust and the tools for living.

From all levels of the office in corporations large and small across the United States, I heard the plea for grown-ups to lead us at work, grown-ups who are givers as well as takers. Grown-ups with a sense of their own worth and awareness of their own weaknesses. Grown-ups who, like wise parents, control their own behavior and, by doing so, discourage childish rebellion and temper tantrums in the subordinates they are trusted to lead.

At work we look into the faces of our bosses, colleagues, and subordinates and see the family we had as children . . . or those we longed for.

Although some of us are aware of this process, we do not always act on it, preferring to believe that our brains, our hard work, and our talent will take us where we want to go. Not so. All around us is the proof. Henry Ford 2nd, according to several printed accounts, fired Lee Iacocca from the Ford Motor Company simply because he just didn't like him. William Paley abandoned three handpicked heirs for his own special reasons (their ambition, it was whispered, proved exasperating to him) before he found one who pleased him sufficiently. Jeane Kirkpatrick has revealed that President Reagan looks on his White House employees as sons, but regards security adviser William Clark as a brother.

Every corporation and every office can supply other examples of personality matches and mismatches that have produced significant career changes. Time and again we have all witnessed hirings and firings based on irrational or inexplicable reasons.

What we lack so desperately and need so urgently is the job description of "grown-up" before the titles of director, president, vice-president, manager, assistant, supervisor. And employee, too.

In the end does it matter, really, whether we play father, mother, son, daughter, sister, or brother? Of course it matters, personally and professionally. The choice will always depend on unexpressed, unresolved needs—theirs and ours. Throughout our lives we play many roles with many people. The more skillful we are at doing this, the more singular our progress is in the corporation. When family roles work to our advantage and we become the favorite son or daughter, we easily understand the truth of family relationships at work. But when we are stepchildren or scapegoats, it is hard to admit the reality of family at work.

There is no equality within the corporate family—as there is no equality among children or between parents, and it is an illusion to wish it so. But there can be justice and respect in the office as there is in the ideal family household. There can be nourishing and nurturing relationships without emotional cruelty.

Family roles in the office are inevitable and often valuable. But we must not allow them to degenerate into the personal and pathological. It is up to us to keep those relationships as adult as humanly possible and not be sucked into someone else's tortured personal needs or allow ourselves to do that to other people, be they boss or subordinate.

We look for love in all the wrong places sometimes, including the office. Asking to be loved, hated, or needed to the limit of endurance (theirs and ours) is asking for neurotic entanglements with the potential to destroy. Asking for respect, justice, and peace in the office is asking for adult friendship, satisfying and sane.

We may find it yet—in the corporate relationships of tomorrow emerging from today's new values.

TEN

Tomorrow's Corporate Family

"Both men and women need to develop behaviors traditionally assigned to the opposite sex. People who possess the best attributes of both sexes will be the leaders in the years ahead."
—JANE EVANS, *vice-president, General Mills*

Back in 1970 I was a researcher at Herman Kahn's think tank, the Hudson Institute, housed in an elegant old mansion overlooking slopes of woods in Croton-on-Hudson, New York.

It was a heady time, politically and personally. The new "women's liberation movement" was struggling for life out of the civil rights marches and the Vietnam War protests. Betty Friedan's *The Feminine Mystique* had been published in 1963, and Ms. Friedan and other women had formed the National Organization for Women in 1966. By 1969 consciousness-raising groups were organizing in New York City. In our suburbs most women remained in their traditional roles of wife, mother, and family chauffeur, but a few were beginning to stir.

Around the mahogany lunch tables in the forbidding and proper dining room, the men of the Hudson Institute snickered at newspaper accounts of those "crazy women's libbers." The women of the Hudson Institute, from the secretaries to the research associates, were wary and sometimes frightened by the rhetoric, but we did not laugh. We were trying to understand it and relate it to our own lives.

I persuaded the Institute that the emerging women's rights movement was an important issue worthy of study in the same way that other social issues (drugs, counterculture, alienation of the young, war protests, campus unrest) were being examined. After exploring all facets of the emerging women's rights movement in my research paper, I discussed the new demands for equality that women were making in 1970. Nearly all were job-related. Among them: day-care centers at work, promotion of significant numbers of women into middle- and upper-level management, equal pay for equal work, flexible working hours, part-time jobs, paraprofessional careers, the abolishment of quotas for women in medical and law schools, and more opportunity for women in the military and the clergy.

Every one of these new ideas—ridiculed, resisted, or unthinkable at the time—would become accepted, approved, then stitched into the fabric of life by the 1980s!

Even by 1977 the mass exodus from home to office was recognized as "a revolution in the roles of women" by Eli Ginzberg, a Columbia University economist and chairman of the National Commission for Manpower Policy. "It is the single most outstanding phenomenon of this century," he told Georgia Dullea of *The New York Times.* "It is a worldwide phenomenon, an integral part of a changing economy and a changing society. Its secondary and tertiary consequences are really unchartable."

The single most outstanding phenomenon of the century. Not a decade, but the full century of one hundred years. Out of all the changes in the world from 1900 to 2000, this is the one with the most lasting impact on society. Not the rise of communism. Not the nuclear bomb. Not the computer. *But the sheer numbers of women at work—* unprecedented in history. And the percentages continue to rise. According to the Women's Bureau, U.S. Department of Labor, 54 percent of women over sixteen were employed or actively seeking jobs in

1984, and they represented 44 percent of the total civilian work force. (When Eli Ginzberg described "a revolution in the roles of women" in 1977, 48.9 percent of women were working, or slightly over 40 percent of the work force. The 1950 figure was 34 percent, or 29.6 percent of the work force.)

By 1990 about 70 percent of U.S. women are expected to be working, and some researchers predict that by 1995, 91 percent of all women ages twenty-five to thirty-four, married, unmarried, with children or without, will be working, representing nearly 50 percent of the work force.

Since those early days of the exodus, women and women's values have changed the ways we work and the ways we think about work. Now they are beginning to change the nature of office relationships between men and women, men and men, and women and women.

As members of professional organizations and women's rights groups, and as individuals, women have helped rewrite corporate policies on male and female job categories, equal pay and promotion, sexual harassment, pensions, insurance, maternity leaves. Focusing the nation's attention on family priorities to benefit men as well as women, they helped create the climate for workplace innovations like company day-care centers, flexible time schedules, job sharing, and part-time work . . . many now in the experimental stages, but models for the future.

Like the men already running the corporate family, in the beginning most women continued the pattern of traditional family relationships they found within the office. They could do nothing else, for they knew nothing else. They were and are mother, daughter, sister, good child, and bad child to father, son, and brother.

But today some women (and men, too) are beginning to reject these roles and to propose a more androgynous style. They believe that corporations would function better if male and female values were integrated into corporate life. Jane Evans, vice-president of General Mills, Inc., responsible for five companies and $650 million worth of business annually, told members of the New York Women in Communications:

"Both men and women need to develop behaviors traditionally assigned to the opposite sex. People who possess the best attributes of both sexes will be the leaders in the years ahead."

Women, she insists, must become powerful, forthright, and more entrepreneurial. They need to learn to generalize from experience and to react more impersonally. Men, on the other hand, must learn to express their feelings and accept the risk of vulnerability implied by this sharing. They must understand the need for comfort and nurturing when they feel hurt, afraid, vulnerable, and helpless, and not hide behind a mask of strength.

"Be tough-minded but not hard-hearted," Ms. Evans advised. "Because business is very competitive, it requires intestinal fortitude and tough, strong-willed individuals. But being tough on the job can become a way of life. Be firm but be fair and have fun."

This is radical advice from one of the first women to reach a high corporate frontier. Revolutionary in its concepts. As revolutionary as the changes in society's attitudes toward women that made it possible. Here is a vice-president of General Mills, one of the country's biggest and most powerful conglomerates, urging women to stop taking everything personally and urging men to start expressing their feelings!

Ms. Evans' is not a lone voice out there, calling for traditional "female" qualities of communication, compassion, and cooperation in the corporate world. This new philosophy of management is advocated by management experts, male and female, in best-selling books and in seminars.

Meantime, current psychological research is beginning to redefine women and explain women's values without the male bias that began with Freud and continued through Jean Piaget, Erik Erikson, and Daniel Levinson.

A major theorist of the new psychology is Dr. Carol Gilligan, psychologist, Harvard associate professor of education and author of *In a Different Voice* (Harvard University Press, 1982). She believes that society has largely ignored women's values in favor of men's because major psychological developmental theory has always taken male experience as the norm.

Men find their identities by separating from their mothers while women achieve their identities in being like their mothers, according to Dr. Gilligan. When men become close, particularly with females, their sense of masculinity may be threatened, she told *The Washington Post*'s Carol Krucoff.

"In a male-female relationship, as the man starts to get scared by the intimacy and move away, the woman starts to get scared by the isolation and get closer," Dr. Gilligan said. Men, who generally fear intimacy, build a system of noninterference involving concepts of justice, fairness, rights. Women, who generally fear separation, feel that people ought to be responsive to each other and responsible for taking care of each other.

Men and women, she says, need to develop each other's views, for the world needs male and female voices. Men should recognize their need for closeness. Women should stop being so self-sacrificing and be more assertive about their own needs.

Female values will continue to change the world of work and the nature of relationships at the office. But the corporate world of the year 2000 will face serious challenges arising from the conflicting demands of three different generations.

Older women, the pioneers who lived the daily revolution in society's expectations for women and in women's expectations for themselves, are now in their mid- and late forties and will be in their sixties by the year 2000. But they will look and act much younger than their mothers did at the same age. Because they have taken such good physical and emotional care of themselves, these women executives will seem to be years younger than they actually are and will want to continue working long past conventional retirement age.

Also by the year 2000, not just the physical gap, but the psychic age gap between a woman of sixty and a man and woman of forty will be narrowed. With less hierarchy and more need for cooperation in corporate life, and with the integration of male and female value systems, women of sixty will feel more like sisters than mothers to men and women of forty and fifty.

But by the year 2000, for the first time in history, a huge and near equal number of educated, talented, ambitious men and women from their fifties to their thirties will be fiercely competing against each other for work. Inevitably, the oldest wave of Baby Boomers, the

"Muppies," will crowd the older women and men off the corporate ladder.

The Baby Boom generation begins with the Muppies, or Middle-age Urban Professionals, born after World War II and now in their thirties.

In 1948 the birth rate skyrocketed to 3,653,921 from 2,868,647 the year before. The boom ended eighteen years later in 1966 with 4,059,898 births.

By the following year, 1967, the birth rate had dropped to 3,782,784 and continued falling until it reached 3,614,000 in 1983. Although the Baby Boom generation is larger in total numbers than any generation in U.S. history, so far it is reproducing itself at record low rates. The number of children per family was about 1.79 in 1983, or two fewer than the 3.72 children per family in 1957.

Muppies are a group in transition, bridging the gap between old values and the new high technology. Ahead of them are the older people in their forties and fifties, still holding some of the traditional attitudes—although they discarded many in the turmoil of the 1960s. Behind the Muppies are the "Yuppies," the Young Urban Professionals in their twenties who control the language and customs of the new computer age.

In the late 1960s and early 1970s the Muppies were in their critical, formative years between ten and twenty—young enough to observe the world, too young to do much about it. They witnessed the most turbulent and frightening years in American history since the Civil War. Theirs is the first TV generation, nurtured on "Romper Room," "I Love Lucy," Ed Sullivan, Alan Shepard, John Glenn, and witnessing the tragedies of John F. Kennedy, Martin Luther King, Robert F. Kennedy. For a while every newscast seemed to bring another assassination, another campus riot, another civil-rights-march killing, another protest rally against the Vietnam War.

Overnight, old rules crumbled, new values surfaced. Parents divorced. Fathers grew long hair and wore chains. Mothers traded aprons for pants suits and started earning their own money. Children were suddenly expected to share the load of laundry and dishes at the same time they were expected to cope with the world around them gone mad. Understandably, they resented these cataclysmic changes.

They grew up frightened by the events they were powerless to understand, much less stop. Reaching adulthood, they seemed reluctant to relinquish those traditional values they had known and had lost. I think that helps explain their political conservatism, their lack of adventure, their longing for stability.

When Muppies, both men and women, grew up and began working, they continued the traditional (male) value system already in place in the office.

Too young during the mid-60s and 1970s to challenge the established order in sex roles, Muppie women reaped windfall benefits from the earlier women's crusades without the work or the pain of revolution.

Some of them wondered what all the fuss had been about. They felt confident that they would get it all and keep it all—the great job at great pay, the great marriage, and, later on, when they found it convenient, the great children. By the mid-1980s they would begin to discover the reality of finite possibilities and narrow choices.

For Muppie women, especially those hearing their biological time clocks, the biggest professional challenge today is the personal one: when to start their own families at home. Some simply drop out of the business world. Some, if they can afford it, hire full-time help at home. Others go into business for themselves. Still others, of course, are content to create their own families around them at work.

The pioneer women who preceded Muppie women at work opened the doors for women and removed much of the financial, legal, educational, and corporate discrimination against them. Still firmly in place, though, for most people, are traditional attitudes about women and "women's place" in life—attitudes that benefit the opposite sex, attitudes that the pioneers so far have not been able to erase.

Muppie men remain resentful of what they see as affirmative action advantages and—the real problem, seldom acknowledged—the doubling of the potential pool of candidates in a huge Baby Boom generation that found the job market as crowded as the schools they usually attended on double sessions.

Confused and conflicted, the Muppies are now caught between old values they mourn and the new technology they mistrust. The generation that witnessed the birth of a new, looser family structure at home is trying to ensure survival of a new, interdependent family framework in the office. It is forging a new philosophy of corporate responsibility in dimensions that go far beyond day-care centers or flexible hours.

Two extraordinary women in their thirties are now beginning to articulate this new family morality in the corporate world.

Both women come from broken homes. Both grew up without their fathers. Both are mavericks, controversial and constantly criticized. Both are intelligent, beautiful, and strong. They are probably the most untypical examples of corporate women in the United States, although they both have excellent traditional business educations. Their careers have been defined by their personal relationships to a father and to a husband, which may have sharpened their vision of corporate responsibility in the future.

They preach a new gospel of corporate caring in their speeches and interviews. Theirs is a message for a world where the only constant is change and where work offers us the stability we have lost at home.

One woman is Christie Hefner, *Playboy* chief operating officer and president of Playboy Enterprises, and the daughter of Hugh Hefner, founder of *Playboy.* The other is Mary Cunningham, former vice-president of strategic planning for Joseph P. Seagram and the former Bendix Company vice-president who resigned amid controversy over her relationship with the chairman, William Agee, whom she later married.

In speeches and in interviews with ABC, *Savvy, Parade, The Washington Post,* and UPI, Mary Cunningham has constantly referred to family values and family situations inside the corporation. When I met her, she assured me that she still felt as strongly as ever about the family as a model in the business world.

A sampler of her public thoughts on the family at work:

• "Bill Agee was going like a father in front of his family to explain things." (Mr. Agee, at a company meeting, said, "It is true that we are very close friends and she is a close friend of my family, but that has nothing to do with the way I and others evaluate her performance.")

• "It is time to consider a new corporate model—one that stresses the importance of human relationships and places the needs of the individual at least alongside those of the institution as a whole."

• "I didn't at the time [at Harvard Business School] imagine myself being necessarily a mother or a married woman. I saw myself, frankly, as a nun of some sort. I have considered the prospect of working with men in a more celibate situation, where I'd be a nun and they'd be priests. Being a member of the Church is a little like being a member of a family—like being a member of that corporation."

• "I suggest that the traditional model for corporate structure is not only outmoded, but is a dangerous time bomb. Imagination and initiative can't be legislated from the top down. The family model is not perfect. But contrast the unselfishness and willingness to go the extra mile that characterizes the family as a unit with the 'What have you done for me lately?' attitude in corporate structures.

• "I don't expect that adoption of the family model will change rightfully competitive workers into hand-holding brothers and sisters. And I don't need to tell anyone that family life isn't always sweetness and light. But beyond the inevitable—and healthy—tensions there is a cohesion and cooperation that most corporations today sadly lack."

• "Business. Sometimes I joke with Bill that it's almost like our child. We share it in common, we nurture it together, we both have opinions about how it should be developed. We've been through a battle together, and we've survived. It's made us stronger."

Playboy's Christie Hefner is also publicly discussing reforms in the corporate way of life, including considering the needs of the individual employee as important as the needs of the corporation. "If you establish a philosophy that people who get ahead are those who are never home with their families, you're not going to have a very healthy company or very healthy workers," she said in a speech quoted by *The Washington Post*.

Playboy has a permanent part-time work force, which includes Ms. Hefner's mother, who works four days a week in the personnel department. The company also offers flexible hours. It gives full-time benefits to part-time employees, recognizing the needs of mothers with young children. "They wanted to continue to have their seniority and profit sharing and access to benefits," Ms. Hefner said, according to the *Post*. "We had the feeling people going through that transition should continue to have their time in the company and their seniority be recognized."

Judy Mann, a *Post* columnist, wrote, "Ms. Hefner points to recent studies showing that corporations that succeed are those that make their employees 'feel that they are part of something bigger than their little job.' She measures the success of the approach against absenteeism, tardiness, the time it takes to do a job, and frequent attitude surveys. 'We have found the more responsibility we give back to employees, the less of those other kinds of bad performance problems occur.'

"Back in the fifties," commented Ms. Mann, "*Playboy* was in the vanguard of the sexual revolution, which, with its emphasis on family planning, helped enable women to go to work. Hefner says that American society has not done anything to reflect the changes and pressures this has created in families.

"But she, at least, is doing her part."

Young men, too, seem to want to change the sterile all-business nature of corporate life into a more human, family enterprise of cohesion and cooperation. For example, David Liederman, founder of David's Cookies in New York, was praised by his employees in a New York *Daily News* article for running his company like a family. He gives them as many sick days and personal days as they need, plus interest-free loans, sizable salary hikes, and lunches at a French restaurant. He also sponsors softball and basketball teams. And he never criticizes one employee in front of another one.

Pioneering corporate women began the revolution in family relationships at the office first by challenging the established order of sex discrimination in business, law, medicine, education, sports, religion.

The revolution in the roles of women has changed the lives of us all, men and women.

Today the pioneers are going even further, daring to challenge the established order of personality traits of both sexes, suggesting that men develop women's sensitivity and that women develop men's toughness. If that idea is accepted (and I believe that is already beginning to be) it will mean much less traditional male-female role-playing and many more egalitarian relationships in the future.

As Muppies pursue the revolution in relationships, they will change the corporate family by daring to ask "Why?":

Why must work rules and company benefits be the same for a new mother and father as they are for parents with grown children? Why can't corporations hire husbands and wives and let them work together as equals? Why is the happiness of an individual employee not as important a goal as success, and why can't business contribute to that happiness—for the good of business?

Muppies realize the urgent need to improve family life and they are beginning to insist that corporate America make room for the experience of birth and parenting, time for reflection, recreation, and rejuvenation—for men and women.

Christie Hefner and Mary Cunningham may well be prophets of the future. At any rate, they are drawing the nation's attention to corporate concerns for families. They are challenging business to develop a coherent philosophy about benefits for all the family. These concepts may well prove as visionary as the idea of the five-day workweek.

Crowding behind the Muppies are the Yuppies, or the Young Urban Professionals, the first generation to incorporate the benefits of high technology into their own lives, using technology but not being used by it.

What is important to remember about Yuppies is their number. Yuppies' birthrates topped over four million each year from 1956 through 1966.

Older Yuppies are much like the Muppies in values and life-styles. But those born in the mid-sixties are too young to recall much about the death and destruction that the Muppies remember from television.

Younger Yuppies' TV memories begin with Watergate and the resignation of their President in disgrace.

Perhaps as a result they are skeptical about politicians, disillusioned about government (often indifferent to voting), disdainful about "quick-fix" solutions to social and political issues, cool, cynical, diffident, less idealistic. They are practical about wanting material comforts, easily bored, with shorter attention spans (blame that on TV) and often inclined toward a certain theatricality (blame that on rock videos).

To Robert Savage, president of Compton Advertising, they are self-centered, lazy, restless—troubled and troubling. In *Media Industry Newsletter,* Mr. Savage acidly described the Baby Boomers, ages eighteen to thirty-six, now one third of the nation's population, this way: "They are the best-educated generation in our history, have more disposable income and more working women than ever before. They also have the highest suicide and divorce rates, and move and change jobs more often.

"The traditional value builders—religion, media, school, textbooks, work, geography, income, family, and friends—have been replaced," he continued. "Unlike previous generations, Boomers' values have been influenced by Dr. Spock, suburbs, sex, drugs, rock 'n' roll, movies, and television. They're more concerned with the self. They seek immediate gratification. They believe in their own group. They're fad-oriented. Outsiders are not welcome. Older generations are not to be trusted. They seek personal freedom and distrust government. They're less committed to work. They're dissatisfied, uncertain, anxious, afraid of the bomb. They are still unsure of their role in society."

Like the Muppies, many Yuppies are children of one-parent families, but unlike the Muppies they are less emotional about it. For them divorce is a somewhat predictable event in most parental lives. In a one-parent household, that one parent at home is usually a mother, which gives children an insight into the problems of working women as nothing else could.

As a group, younger Yuppies tend to be more emotionally secure than older Yuppies and the Muppies. Younger Yuppies are also more experimental, take more risks in their personal lives, and are interested in spiritualism, even the occult.

At work they are confident about their abilities, even cocky, but many are getting the reputation for needing a lot of feedback and hand-holding. They also tend to drag their personal problems into work, some bosses complain. (Making the office their home?)

They want a quick evaluation of their work and their chances for a promotion. They are intensely competitive, ambitious, pragmatic, job hoppers, with little interest in job security or pension plans and little loyalty to the company or the product.

They want what they want when they want it—which is usually now.

Women Yuppies at work today, many with working mothers and certainly with more women as role models than ever before, are assertive, independent in their personal relationships, realistic about planning their careers and lifetime goals, determined to get their share.

Yuppie men feel easier than their older brothers and certainly their fathers did around women at work. Still, in their heart of hearts, they appear reluctant to relinquish the traditional male prerogatives no matter what their heads tell them.

If they are two-career couples, Yuppies often try to work out equal opportunities for each other when the baby comes. The wife opens her own business, either as a consultant or free-lance from her home, or starts a company near home. Or they alternate career priorities (she supports him in graduate school, he promises to relocate). Or else they resolve it with the traditional your-career-is-more-important-than-mine decision (usually the more important and lucrative career is the man's). Occasionally, they both try for career equality, which is practically impossible to achieve without money for around-the-clock help.

Many Yuppies are still in colleges, universities, and graduate schools, and those at work have just begun their careers, so they have had little opportunity to change corporate relationships as yet. But they will as they get older.

As the largest age cohort group in American history, they will be fierce competitors, with men and women as equals or nearly so, as they have been from the first days of nursery school. As a result, instead of today's sibling rivalry, young men and women of the corporation will compete mostly in teams. This is already beginning to happen.

They will continue to be rather indifferent to all forms of authority, from their labor union president or their professional association president to their company president. I say this after talking to my young friends in young industries, like computer programming and consulting. They report that their twenty-eight-year-old company president or thirty-two-year-old vice-president sees himself as a trouble-shooter and adviser and treats them as cousins. In contrast, the more traditional firms they do business with (banking, importing) maintain the hierarchy of father, son, and daughter relationships.

Young Urban Professionals insist on more control over their work and leisure time, and usually get it. With their mastery of the computer and their intense self-confidence, even before they begin to run corporate America, they will create their own options, dropping in, dropping out at will during various stages of their careers. The new technology, linking home to office by computers, will allow them to do this.

By the year 2000 about a third of the work force in industrialized countries will no longer commute to the office but use a computer terminal at home. Half of all managers and executives will use electronic work stations. These predictions were made by a panel of sixteen of the world's leading futurists at a general assembly of the Washington-based World Future Society. The panel also predicted that 71 percent of the work force in industrialized countries will work in the information and communications sector of the economy by the year 2000, an increase over the estimated 50–55 percent today.

Commenting on the future for *Editor & Publisher,* Dr. Leo Bogart, executive vice-president and general manager of the Newspaper Advertising Bureau, said, "The division of labor between the sexes will be progressively less distinct. . . . With a growing population of vigorous older people, the definitions of work and leisure will be blurred. The relationship between home and the workplace will be different, as home communications systems allow more personal business, shopping, and work activity to take place at home."

Several futurists believe that more work will be managed by workers and the workplace itself will become more cooperative than adversarial. At a conference on work held by the World Future Society they predicted that education will become the largest industry (replacing today's health-care and medicine) because the huge number of Baby Boomers will need to be retrained as new needs and new jobs replace old ones. "We will change careers every ten years and need retreading in basic communication and English, reading and logic," said futurist David Snyder, a conference speaker. "The goal will be to achieve competence and avoid dependence on the system."

Because over a lifetime Yuppies will start and stop many different jobs, they will start and stop relationships with many different people —who will become more like aunts and uncles, cousins and stepsisters and stepbrothers, than the closer-knit ties of today's mother, father, son, daughter, sister, and brother.

Tomorrow, as today, the office will reflect the home. If tomorrow's home has the extended in-law family relationships of shifting, impermanent, essentially transient relationships of family members, so will the office.

By the year 2000 pioneers will be in their sixties and on their way out. Their legacy will live on in all the ways we think about women that are totally different from the way we thought in 1970. Their legacy will live on in the more egalitarian and androgynous office, where there will be less time or inclination for sex roles, sex-defined personalities, or surrogate family members. Where there will be as well (we hope) equal pay for equal work and for work of equal worth, which will be an increasingly important office issue. In the year 2000, Muppies will be in their forties and fifties and will be managing the corporations of America. Still nostalgic for old-fashioned family values, they will improve working conditions and options for men and women, offering flexible hours, increased or full benefits for part-time work, medical and life insurance tailored to individual requirements, and more consultants jobs (enabling both sexes to drop in and out of the work force as family duties and personal needs dictate).

The pioneers expanded the professional opportunities for women. The Muppies will expand professional and personal opportunities with a smorgasbord of options for all employees.

When the Yuppies take over corporate America by 2020 they will expand the role of the corporation in the emotional life of its employees. Executives and managers will need greater communications skills than ever before because so many employees will be at home, in the electronic cottage, isolated and lonely. Home will be more like the office, and the office will become more like home used to be—a place to be with the "family" and be involved in a myriad of relationships, if only for a short time. Tomorrow's successful executives may be the ones with skills to make home-based employees who come to the office only periodically feel like part of a "family."

Yuppies will have fewer children, later in life. Instead of knowing one set of parents, those children will know several types of "parents" —nurses, baby-sitters, teachers, and (if present trends continue) a sequence of stepparents. The idea of "mother" and "father" will be less authoritative and more egalitarian.

The family will change, as it always does. Family-type feelings, the need for support, nurturing, love, intimacy, and drama will remain, as they always do. These needs will be met in different ways, by different people, in different places. As always, the office will be one of those places.

As divorce continues to separate so many couples, the breakup of the traditional family, followed by subsequent remarriages and stepfamilies, will profoundly affect family-type relationships at work.

Those who learned to get along successfully with stepparents, stepsiblings, and stepchildren of their own will find it easy and professionally advantageous to cultivate superficial but friendly relationships at work.

As we live longer more of us will divorce and remarry, or simply live with someone. In the sequential marriage and living-together arrangements of the late twentieth century, the emotional bonds will be weaker between many fathers and sons, fathers and daughters, mothers and sons, mothers and daughters. But the bonds will often be stronger among siblings and stepsiblings who draw close to each other for security and for understanding. For this reason, the brother-sister feeling will be the strongest office relationship for most people in the future.

Increasing numbers of children will come of age in one-parent homes (in 1983, 22 percent of all children under eighteen lived with only one parent, up from 11.9 percent in 1970), then perhaps later on, stepparent homes. Consequently, the forty-year-olds of the year 2000 will be, from an early age, more self-reliant, sophisticated, responsible, and independent, as nonchalant about cooking dinner as they are about changing tires and diapers.

In the more equal, participatory corporate atmosphere of the year 2000, executives will not be allowed to stand much on ceremony, or title, or status, nor will subordinates be permitted the luxury of acting out so many family-role games—if, indeed, they know how. Old, rigid "Father knows best" management styles will be replaced by a brisker "Let's do it together" point of view already operating in the younger firms, notably those in the computer industry. This is partly a reaction to foreign management successes, especially the Japanese, partly a reaction to changing relationships at home, and partly a reaction to the more freewheeling attitudes of younger employees. In time most office relationships will become more interdependent instead of dependent, with less clearly differentiated sex roles.

Today's corporate family is headed by a "father" who finds the child he never had, the child he always wanted at the office, and guides him (sometimes her) up the ladder.

Tomorrow's corporate family will be headed by a man or a woman —not necessarily in the old-fashioned father or mother role, but more an adult friend, a protector and adviser to his or her adult children, cousins, siblings, and stepsiblings. We will be grown-ups working with grown-ups, but still fulfilling our own individual, special emotional needs.

Corporations, seeing themselves in new roles with new responsibilities, will offer us more professional and personal options. Our work will become more central to our well-being and the key to our stability in an erratic world.

I expect that office relationships will turn out to be more equal, more caring, and more fun in more limited periods of time. So what if we change careers every decade or so? We'll have more tries at the brass ring. Just as we do today, we may find the family we never had, family we always wanted.

And it is good to belong.

_ol